The CHURCH in America is Dying...

But is All Hope Lost?

REV. JACK MUNLEY

Copyright © 2014 by Rev. Jack Munley

The Church in America is Dying...But is All Hope Lost?
by Rev. Jack Munley

Edited by Xulon Press

Front cover artist by Barbara Sick

Photography of Back cover by Jenn Ruggiero

Printed in the United States of America

ISBN 9781498411493

All rights reserved solely by the author. The author guarantees all contents are original and do not infringe upon the legal rights of any other person or work. No part of this book may be reproduced in any form without the permission of the author. The views expressed in this book are not necessarily those of the publisher.

Scripture quotations, unless stated otherwise, are taken from the New King James Version (NKJV). Copyright © 1997 by Thomas Nelson, Inc.

www.xulonpress.com

Table of Contents

Chapter 1. A Disease Called SIN 7
Chapter 2. A Garment of Iniquity........................14
Chapter 3. Jesus Desires to Restore His Church ..22
Chapter 4. Revelation Churches 29
Chapter 5. Searching the Deep Things of God.....37
Chapter 6. The Pharisaical Church......................44
Chapter 7. The Church of Dry Bones...................53
Chapter 8. The Work of the Holy Spirit
is Missing..61
Chapter 9. The Church is Defenseless 68
Chapter 10. Where are Our Weapons of Warfare?.75
Chapter 11. Friendship with the World or God? 86
Chapter 12. Genesis of Sin.....................................99
Chapter 13. Do We View the World Through
God's Lenses or Man's? 115
Chapter 14. God's Desire for Visitation
in His Church 130
Chapter 15. Cure for Sin 147
Chapter 16. A Transplanted Heart 153
Chapter 17. Biblical Love 168
Chapter 18. The Attributes of God's Love 174
Chapter 19. Applying God's Love 195
Chapter 20. Worldly Love vs. Godly Love 207
Chapter 21. Love Is the Answer...........................222
Chapter 22. All Hope Is Not Lost 241

Chapter 1
A Disease Called SIN

The church in America is dying. A disease has infiltrated the entire church and is progressively getting worse. It's contagious, crippling, and so insidious it's threatening the spread of the Gospel in this country and could cause the extinction of the church in America. This horrible disease is called SIN.

Sin, or as I like to describe it, "self-indulgent need," is pervasive and choking the life out of the church in America. What is the church? Is the church a building or a group of believers who gather together as one? Focus on the Family wrote a compelling article about the definition of the church. Some people view the church as a building where people gather to worship on Sundays, but church is much more than a building, biblically speaking. "In fact, some would say that the church is not a building at all, but is all about the people. But what is the church?" The article states that the early Christian church didn't consist of buildings but a group of people who met secretly for fear of persecution. "As Christianity spread, eventually buildings dedicated to worship were established and became what we know today as churches. In this sense, then, the church consists of people, not buildings. The focus of this book is how or the manner in which the church, the people, are failing God miserably.

Sin is excused and permitted from the pulpit and is no longer crouching at the door, as God warned Cain when He told him, *"If you do not do well, sin lies at the door. And its desire is for you, but you should rule over it." (Gen. 4:7)* It has now sneaked into the church and is sitting in the pews every Sunday under the guise of church membership, money, tolerance, acceptance, and greed. Sin's desire is for every person; its goal is to destroy the church from within.

Sin is hardly preached from the pulpit anymore, much to the anger and dismay of God. It has been usurped by the prosperity gospel and anything else that people's itching ears want to hear, because we want to feel good, our self-indulgent needs satisfied. Desire has already been conceived since it has made its way inside of the church and now has given birth to sin. James 1:15 states, *"when it is full grown, it brings forth death."* It's not just physical death, but spiritual death as well.

The church in America is spiritually sick and is dying on its bed of iniquity, cut off from the healing touch and forgiveness of Christ despite some churches experiencing record numbers. The church is supposed to be a place where sin-laden people come for repentance, forgiveness for their sins, a change of heart to take place, and then a new, vibrant life birthed for the glory of God. However, the exact opposite has taken place because we're either spiritually blinded to the truth of the Gospel or just don't care because people are here, filling up our church pews. Do we not care that those very people are destined to hell because of their sin?

Pastors have turned away from sound doctrine because it's what their members demand. They have turned to their own desires, and have now turned their ears away from the truth and turned aside to fables. (2 Tim. 4:3-5). Isn't that what sin does? It turns us from the living God, from the truth, from the cross where sin was nailed and where it all begins and ends, all to satisfy our fleshly desires and needs.

Instead of bringing Christ from the church and into the world and society, we have brought the world, along with its selfish desires and needs, into the church. And it's a cancer that's spreading! God is bringing judgment and His judgment is righteous and true. We're asleep like the disciples were in the Garden of Gethsemane when Jesus asked them to pray and be on guard; we're not sober and vigilant to eradicate the sin in our lives. Sin is contagious and is even affecting those who do come to church every week, who are seeking Him and His desire for their lives. Their spirit is indeed willing but their flesh is weak. They can't gain control over their sin because they don't know how to. It has gotten its grip upon them. They're not taught the sound doctrine Christ demands we teach each other. They can't tell the difference between good and evil anymore because all forms of self-indulgent needs are accepted.

The Barna Group Ltd., which conducts primary research, produces media resources pertaining to spiritual development, and facilitates the healthy spiritual growth of leaders, children, families and Christian ministries, conducted a study in 2008 titled, "A New Generation of Adults Bends Moral and Sexual Rules to Their Liking," focused on the difference between those in their twenties and thirties, an age group comprised primarily of the so-called "Buster" generation, and those over the age of forty. Among "born-again" Busters, a label based upon their beliefs about Jesus Christ and regarding life after death, 59 percent polled agreed that cohabitation is morally acceptable, while 65 percent of non-Christian older adults agreed and

80 percent of non-Christian Busters concurred. "The same response pattern was evident when it came to gambling, sexual fantasies, abortion, sex outside of marriage, profanity, pornography, same-sex marriage, and the use of illegal drugs." The church in America is failing its people as the world has influenced the church. The article continues, "Busters have a more disconnected, individualized, less trusting spin on morality. They are trying to create a sense of identity because they feel the shaping influences such as family, church, and community has failed them."

Currently, traditional biblical marriage between one man and one woman is under attack and the church is sitting idly by or even agreeing with the world's trend towards acceptance of same-sex relationships and marriages. In 2003 69 percent of practicing Christians under the age of forty and 73 percent of practicing Christians over the age of forty agreed that marriage is defined as one man and one woman. However, in 2013 the numbers have fallen to 61 percent and 70 percent respectively. Also, in 2003 22 percent of practicing Christians under the age of forty and 11 percent over the age of forty considered same-sex sexual relationships to be morally acceptable. However, in 2013 the numbers have jumped to 25 percent and 18 percent respectively among those who now believe that same-sex sexual relationships to be morally acceptable.

More Christians are getting divorced than ever before. Some couples are attending church faithfully but living together in sin, as they are not married. Adultery and sexual immorality are rampant, homosexuality is an accepted practice and considered not sinful. We accept the murder of unborn babies, and it's all excused and not spoken about, because we don't want to offend anybody. We desire to be politically correct instead of preaching the truth found in the Bible because we don't want our members to leave the church. But unless the truth is preached, then to what gain is it to have them forfeit their very souls to eternal damnation because of their sin?

Chapter 2

A Garment of Iniquity

Do we really believe that Christ is happy with the church in America? We are not offering a sweet-smelling sacrifice to God, but a stench that has wafted to His very nostrils, and He is not happy. He requires obedience, not just church attendance every week. We have become a culture not only desensitized to sin, but we have fully embraced it. We have willingly clothed ourselves with its garment and proudly display it for all to see, thinking it's acceptable to God. Instead, it's a moth-eaten, decaying, stench-filled garment that continues to destroy us spiritually. God revealed to the prophet Zechariah in the book of Zechariah 3:2

His thoughts about this garment of sin when, "He showed me Joshua the high priest standing before the angel of the Lord, and Satan standing at his right hand to oppose him. And the Lord said to Satan, 'The Lord rebuke you Satan! The Lord who has chosen Jerusalem rebuke you! Is this not a brand plucked from the fire?'" Now Joshua was clothed with filthy garments, and was standing before the Angel. The Lord commanded those who were standing before Him to "take away the filthy garments from him." And to him He said, "See, I have removed your iniquity from you, and I will clothe you with rich robes."

But the garment of iniquity continues to remain on those in the church today, from the pulpit to the pews, and they refuse to allow the Lord to remove the iniquity from them. They are filthy and the Lord wants to remove the soiled garment from them and replace it with His rich robe of righteousness, but Satan himself stands as our accuser and those in the church continue to listen to him despite his rebuke from our Almighty God! God saved His people, the Israelites, countless times despite their sin-filled ways and desire to do things as they saw fit, but they never got to experience the Promised Land because of their sin, their disobedience, and it's the same in the church today. Do we want to jettison our Promised Land, eternal life in heaven with God, for the temporary pleasures of this life? The truth is distorted for their own evil desires and gain. How many times do people choose certain Scriptures and take them out of context, just to make them feel worthy or accepted or justified in their own eyes, and not God's? They are too numerous to count, and this grieves our Heavenly Father.

God warned us of this happening and why He, in His infinite wisdom, requires and charges us to "preach the Word!" Keep your sense of urgency {stand by, be at hand and ready}, whether the opportunity seems to be favorable or unfavorable. Whether it is convenient or inconvenient, whether it is welcome or unwelcome, you as a preacher of the Word are to show people in what way their lives are wrong. *"And convince them, rebuking, and correcting, warning and urging and encouraging them, being unflagging and inexhaustible in patience and teaching." 2 Tim. 4:2 AMP.*

But the church, sadly, is inconvenienced. His Word is unwelcome and unfavorable to them because of their hardness of heart. But God's judgment is coming and coming swiftly, because the church isn't ready as a bride readies herself for her bridegroom. The bride (the church) has left her bridegroom at the altar, refusing to marry Him and be joined to Him, but has chosen a different bridegroom who is waiting for her at the altar of sin. This bridegroom whispers his lies and deceits into our waiting, itching ears and we believe every word that comes from his poisonous lips because it's what we want to hear. However, it never satisfies our unquenchable thirst for our fleshly desires.

Could it be that we'd be rejected by our bridegroom anyway because of the garment we bring to the altar of the wedding feast? Jesus spoke of the wedding feast in Matthew 22; of a guest who attended the wedding feast without a garment. When he was questioned, he couldn't utter a single word as to why he was unprepared to meet his king. What was the king to do with his guest? Would he excuse his lack of preparation, his brazen attendance at the feast just to attend? Should he excuse his behavior because he didn't follow the king's invitation as written? He attended, right? Isn't that important enough? I attend church every week. I sing the worship songs played; I listen to the sermon preached; I even get involved with church activities from time to time, but I live my life the way I see fit, so I'm okay, right? My Righteous King will accept me anyway because at least I'm here, won't He? The answer is a resounding NO!

The king in the parable ordered that the guest be bound by his hands and feet and cast into the outer darkness, where there was weeping and gnashing of teeth! What? I'll be thrown out into the darkness? Why, how dare He? The visitor had been invited to the wedding, but he had not prepared himself for it. He did not wear the king's garment, a clean garment that was acceptable to the king. To the king who invited you to a wedding feast, it's insulting for you to enter with soiled garments and expect to be accepted.

Isn't it the same with the church today? We insult Christ because we come to church week after week with our soiled, sin-filled garments, and expect Him to accept those garments. We attend just to attend, as the king's guest did. He, the King of Kings and the Lord of Lords, has prepared for us His white garment of righteousness, washed in His blood. Just as the natural king rejected his visitor and had him cast out of the party, Jesus will do the same with us as His invited guests at His banquet table if we don't repent of our sin and wear His garment. His garment is the acceptable garment with which we need to adorn ourselves.

Those who refuse to wear His garment by wearing their own garment, or think it's not necessary to wear

His, are among those who reject the work of Jesus on the cross and His atonement for their sins. The garment of righteousness was provided to us by His sacrificial death upon the cross at Calvary. If we want to enter Christ's banquet, His kingdom, then we need to put on His righteousness. As the guest was thrown out of the banquet hall because he wasn't prepared, those living with their own garments of sin will not be accepted by Jesus either at His feast to come! Isaiah spoke to God's chosen people, the Israelites, as the anointed one of God when he said to His people, "I will greatly rejoice in the Lord, my soul shall be joyful in my God; for he has clothed me with the garments of salvation, He has covered me with the robe of righteousness, as a bridegroom decks himself with ornaments, and as a bride adorns herself with her jewels" (Isa. 61:10 NKJV).

We are supposed to be the bride readying herself for her bridegroom at the altar of salvation, not the altar of sin. He has prepared for us a beautiful garment: a clean, undefiled, unblemished, acceptable garment, and not the stench-filled, sin-riddled, moth-eaten garment that's been laid up by Satan himself. When God was speaking about the restoration of His people and the rebuilding of Jerusalem, He spoke to the prophet Isaiah and said, "Lift up your eyes, look around and see; All these gather together and come to you. As I live says the Lord, you shall surely clothe yourselves with them all as an ornament, and bind them on you as a bride does" (Isa. 49:18 NKJV). Zion's returning people were a splendid ornament, like the jewels of a bride.

Chapter 3

Jesus Desires to Restore His Church

*J*esus wants to restore the church in America too. He so desires that we be like that splendid ornament: clean and undefiled. In the church today, Jesus desires us to be just as beautiful as the jewels on a bride on her wedding day. He wants to gather us as one and return to Him, as His people returned to Him through the prophet Isaiah.

Jesus Christ gave Himself for us, the church, but what have we done to His sacrifice? He has chosen us to be His voice in this sin-filled world, but His voice has been slowly silenced by the metastasis of sin in the church! Christ desires to marry us as He loves the church and *"gave Himself for her, so that He might sanctify her, having cleansed her by the washing of the water with the Word, that He might present to Himself the church in all her glory, having no spot or wrinkle or any such thing; but that she would be holy and blameless." (Eph. 5:26-27) NASB.*

Jesus declares that He "might" sanctify and present the church to Him, not that He will do it, because it is up to us as His bride, His church, to be sanctified and cleansed by Him by choosing to marry Him and thus becoming one with Him. He has asked for permission or liberty to do this. It reminds me of when God had spoken to His chosen people, the Israelites, and told them, *"I have set before you life and death, blessings and curses. Now choose life, so that you and your children may live." (Deut. 30:19) NIV.* It's our choice, our decision. We either choose to allow Him into the church and thus our lives, or we don't. We know the rewards and consequences of our decisions. Our rewards as a church are tremendous blessings and promised eternity with Him!

However, our consequences are also an eternity, yes: an eternity forever without Him! We will be a cursed people forever!

Look at Christ's promise to us as His church: He first wants to sanctify us. To sanctify is to set us apart or declare us holy. We're so special to God that He wants to set us apart, both individually and corporately, for His good purpose and promises. He has chosen us, but the crucial question is: Have we chosen Him?

He then, after setting us apart or sanctifying us, wants to cleanse us. To be cleansed is to be washed, not just on the outside, but from the inside out. God's cleansing purifies us, prepares us for what's in store for Him and with Him. It's not just any cleansing, but a cleansing of the washing of the water with the Word. What Word? His Word, the written Word who became flesh! Jesus Christ *"was the Word and the Word was with God, and the Word was God. He was with God in the beginning. Through Him all things were made; without Him nothing was made that has been made." (Jn. 1:1-3) NIV.*

Jesus is also our living water, the only source of water we need to survive spiritually. He tells us to drink of Him, for He is the source of life, our very sustenance without which we can't survive. And if we drink, we'll never thirst again! *"But whoever drinks the water I give him will never thirst. Indeed the water I give him will become in him a spring of water welling up to eternal life." (Jn. 4:14) NIV.* Jesus also said, *"If anyone thirsts, let him come to Me and drink. He who believes in Me, as the Scripture has said, out of his heart will flow rivers of living water." (Jn.7:37B-38). NKJV.*

He promises that out of our heart, rivers of living water will flow, touching, affecting, and changing those lives around us for eternity. It leaves others the opportunity to drink and be satisfied of Him. It's fresh and fulfilling, as His water never goes stale, but He is the *"same yesterday and today, and forever." (Heb. 13:8) NIV.*

Once we're sanctified and cleansed, He wants to present us, the church, to Himself in all our glory, without spot or wrinkle, holy and blameless! He prepares His bride to meet the bridegroom. But we must then ask ourselves: Is that what's evident in the church in America today? Is she the bride prepared to meet her bridegroom? Is she without spot or wrinkle, holy and blameless? Sadly, the answer is no. We're not set apart to be used by Him, but we're set apart to serve the world and all its evil desires and sin. The world has considered sin acceptable and pleasurable and worthy to indulge in. The world teaches that if it feels right, then why not participate in it? We are to live our own lives in the way that we determine is right and wrong, not the church, right? And all the while we live lives that are only pleasing to ourselves and the world in which we live, and have unfortunately brought that lifestyle into the church. How then can we expect God to be pleased? How can we expect Him to bless our lives? How can we expect Him to answer our prayers? He's not and He won't!

"You [are like] unfaithful wives [having illicit affairs with the world and breaking your marriage vow to God]! Do you not know that being the world's friend is being God's enemy? So whoever chooses to be a friend of the world takes his stand as an enemy of God." (Jas. 4:4) AMP.

James was talking about people in the church who constantly wage a war within themselves that comes from their desire for pleasure and their desire to do God's will. But he chastises those in the church for praying for situations that are not in God's will. And we wonder why He doesn't answer our prayers. We ask amiss because our prayers aren't seeking God's will for our lives but for our will that we want Him to fulfill!

James calls those who practice sin in church adulterers and adulteresses! We have cheated on God within the church. We have been unfaithful to Him and have prostituted ourselves on the altar of sin for all to see. The church is filled with spiritual adulterers and adulteresses, masquerading as angels of light. His Word is clear that friendship with the world is enmity with God. Enmity is the state or feeling of being actively opposed or hostile to someone or something. We oppose, hate, or are hostile to God when the world and its sin are brought into the church. The church has a clear choice to make and it's either friendship with the world or friendship with our Savior Jesus Christ. We can't have it both ways. It's His way and will for our lives, or it's our way. *"And if it seems evil unto you to serve the Lord, choose you this day whom you will serve... but as for me and my house, we will serve the Lord." (Josh. 24:15) KJV.*

The choice is ours to make, but we need to make a choice. Whom will we serve?

Chapter 4

Revelation Churches

*L*et's take a look at what Jesus has to say about those who are in the church and want to have it both ways. They serve God one day and Satan with their own self-indulgent needs, the next. The church in America has become much like the Laodicean church spoken about when Christ revealed it to John in the Book of Revelation. Laodicea was a very wealthy city, as we are in America today. It boasted of prosperous banks, a textile industry, and a medical school. It was a wealthy city by any standard, but Jesus admonished them for their lukewarm attitude within the church. *"I know your works, that you are neither cold nor hot. I could wish that you*

were cold or hot. So then, because you are lukewarm, and neither cold nor hot, I will vomit you out of my mouth." (Rev. 3:15-16) NKJV.

Laodicea was also known for its limited water supply. Its water was lukewarm. Cold water is refreshing and hot water is used for medicinal purposes, but lukewarm water is useless. It serves no purpose. Because they were rich physically, they felt they were in want for nothing, that everything was fine. Jesus was not happy with their half-heartedness, their lack of passion for the things of God, their laziness, their sin! They were narcissistic and egotistical because of their immense material wealth and their personal accomplishments and standing in society, so that they mistakenly thought they were fine. However, they were spiritually famished and self-deluded; they did indeed have a sparse water supply, they weren't connected to Jesus Himself, the true, refreshing, and limitless water.

Because people come to church in their finest garments and tithe weekly, they believe that God is pleased. Is that what He said? He said He would vomit those people out of His mouth. What a graphic judgment the Lord has pronounced upon the church that's lukewarm and not on fire for Him. He will simply regurgitate you, for your deeds that aren't pleasing to Him, for your acceptance of the rampant sins spreading in your church like a cancer, all in the name of religious political correctness instead of your acceptance of Him, His Word and what He desires of His church and His people!

And there are some churches in America just like the church in Ephesus who abandoned their first love — Jesus Christ! We have deserted Him because of sin that's taken the place of Christ on the throne. The church no longer does the works of the Lord that they first did when those church doors opened and all were on fire for Him. That fire spread rapidly in the church affecting positively everyone who entered its doors. But the church became stale. It began to look for ways to make it exciting again. They usurped God's will and plan and replaced it with a worldly viewpoint, leaving Christ behind at His altar; changing their garments and replacing them with their own garments to meet their own evil desires and needs.

The church continues on as if they're operating in His will because people are being saved, the calendars are filled with activities, church membership is up, but the true life-saving Gospel that raises those souls to become Christ-like in His character and deeds isn't preached from the pulpit or in Bible study classes or in the youth groups. He commands that church to return to their first love, to rekindle the fire that burned out, by repenting of their wicked ways and returning to Him, their first love, their first desire. He knew that the church wasn't the same because of the sin that entered it. Where sin exists and reigns, Christ's love is non-existent; it's not welcome.

Perhaps the church in America is like the church described in Pergamos — the church that compromises. Pergamos, which means "Citadel" in Greek, was the ancient capital of the province of Asia. It was a city that sat on a high hill that dominated the valley below. The church at Pergamos was chastened by Christ because it compromised its values. He said it was a church where Satan's throne was, a place where he dwelled. A throne is a ceremonial chair fit for a king or for someone in high regard or standing. In the abstract sense, it's said to be the crown itself and expressions of "the power behind the throne." But the church at Pergamos, according to Christ, had allowed Satan to take up residence upon this throne, to wear the crown himself, to give him the power over their lives right from within the church! *"I know your works, and where you dwell, where Satan's throne is." (Rev. 2:13) NKJV.*

Satan's authority and power were honored quite openly and effectively and all of the members felt all was well. In fact, it was quite the opposite, as those in the church were adhering to the doctrine of Balaam. Balak, who was a king of Moab, hired Balaam, who was a non-Israelite and prophet, to turn the hearts of Israel away from God. Balaam sabotaged the Israelites as they entered the Promised Land and he taught the king how he could turn the Israelites away from God — engage in sexual immorality with prostitutes and have them eat unclean food that was sacrificed to idols. They gave into their temptations and their evil desires and sinned.

Jesus was saying that the church allowed these practices and they are happening in the church in America today, but pastors and fellow members sit idly by and let it happen. They're concerned about their own walk of faith. They focus on those members who give generously every week, while God's throne has been usurped by Satan himself, who laughs and derides Christ right from within His own body! Sexual immorality continues unbridled, the food we eat isn't the life-sustaining food of Jesus Christ, but it's the food of Satan, which is any form of idol worship in our lives that serves Satan and not God. It's any of our daily activities, dreams, goals, or desires that dominate our time, leaving very little or no time for the Lord Himself. Jesus demands repentance in the church for these sins or *"He will come quickly and will fight against them with the sword of My mouth." (Rev. 2:16.) NKJV.*

The next church mentioned in Revelation was the church in Thyatira. Thyatira was a city with a large military detachment, about thirty miles southeast of Pergamos. It was famous for its wool and dye industries. Jesus mentions that this church performed its works, love, service, faith, and patience, and that it was doing more works then than it did in the beginning. Many churches are like that today. Its works were expressed daily, especially in its many ministries dispersed into the community, but Christ still had a few things against this church. It was much like the church at Pergamos because of its sexual immorality and eating food sacrificed to idols. It wasn't thoroughly cleansed or prepared to meet her Lord.

The church was guilty of having its own Jezebel allowed into its ranks within the church. Jezebel was an exceedingly evil woman, who had strong influence over her husband and king, Ahab. Her name means "Lacking Honor," as she used her abilities of great competence and power to dishonor God. There are many who "lack honor" but have great influence over the pastor in their church because they tithe the most or perhaps chair a board.

He has given His church today time to repent of her sins, but she does not. He promises to cast her onto a sickbed for her sin, but isn't she already there? The church is on its sickbed of sin, having great tribulation in the life of her people within her church because of her unconfessed sin. The only remaining end for those on their sickbed of sin is their eternal, spiritual death, an eternity separated from God!

Chapter 5

Searching the Deep Things of God

*J*esus is the one who searches the minds and hearts of those in His church. Do we really think those with unconfessed sin within the church are hidden from God? He promises to give to each of us according to our works. *"But I, the Lord, search all hearts and examine secret motives. I give all people their due rewards, according to what their actions deserve." (Jer.17:10). NLT.* What are our secret motives behind our sin? What do we hope to gain by indulging in it? He clearly rewards us according to what our actions deserve. The church needs to arise from its sickbed of iniquity, repent of its evil ways, be washed clean by His blood, to be renewed with His clean garment of righteousness, and begin their faith walk anew!

There was considerable satanic influence in Asia Minor as there is considerable satanic influence within the church in America today. Instead of being influenced by the "depths of Satan," we should be searching the deep things of God. The church lacks the spiritual wisdom of God because they wrongfully believe that their own wisdom is, in fact, wisdom. However, wisdom apart from God is not wisdom at all, but folly. *"There is a way {man's wisdom} that seems right to a man, but its end is the way of death." (Prov.14:12) NKJV.* We feel that there is a way that is right for us, because it feels good, everybody else is doing it, the pastor hasn't condemned me for it, and so it must be okay. I'm not harming anybody, so why can't I indulge in this sin? It really seems and feels right, doesn't it? But it's not right. It leads to death. We need to search the deep things of God and submit to Him and His wisdom concerning every matter of our lives.

1 Corinthians 2:10 teaches us, *"But God has revealed it to us by His Spirit. The Spirit searches all things, even the deep things of God." NIV.* It's the Holy Spirit, the Third Person of the Trinity, who reveals the deep things of God to us. The deep things of God are not achieved through or own knowledge. We don't take credit for that. It's the indwelling of the Holy Spirit that we receive from Him when we're born again, and have been given that new life He so preciously and freely gives us that leads and guides and directs us into all truth. *"For what man knows the things of a man except the spirit of the man which is in Him? Even so no one knows the things of God except the Spirit of God. Now we have received, not the spirit of the world, but the Spirit who is from God, that we might know the things that have been freely given to us by God." (1 Cor.2:11-12) NKJV.* WE cannot know the things of God unless His Holy Spirit reveals them to us. If sin is revealed, it needs

to be dealt with severely and quickly. He even tells us that we, who are in Him, haven't received the spirit of the world, but the Spirit of God. Jesus was speaking about His people, the born again believers, and the believers who accepted His sacrificial death upon the cross, who accepted the blood He shed on the cross for their sins. But, sadly, the spirit of the world, Satan himself, is the one leading many people in the church today into deception and sin and eventually spiritual death.

If we choose to wear the garment of the spirit of the world, it's impossible to know and search the things of God. We're not free to know all that exists within us from Him because we're enslaved and beholden to the greatest deceiver and liar of all. We are "free" to do his bidding and not God's. We have, in fact, removed the garment of righteousness given to us by Christ through His redemptive work on the cross, and replaced it with the garment of unrighteousness. *"Do you not know that to whom you present yourselves slaves to obey, you are that one's slaves whom you obey, whether of sin leading to death, or of obedience leading to righteousness?"* (Rom. 6:16) NKJV.

The Amplified Bible talks about one who "continually" surrenders oneself to anyone to do his will. It's not referencing an act of sin or disobedience, and neither is God. It's talking about continually and habitually sinning and disobeying God in our words and deeds every day. Continual means "to do something constantly, unceasingly, always happening, without interruption." It becomes our way of life; it's habitual. We have become spiritually blinded and hardened and a slave to Satan because of our constant acts of disobedience and, thus a slave to sin.

If one was a slave to a master in ancient times, he was owned by that master. Whether slaves obeyed their master or not, it didn't change their status as slaves but affected the relationship with their master, as Jesus was talking about in Luke 19:20-26 when He spoke about the parable of the minas. One servant truly didn't fear his master or understand him and didn't do as he was told, resulting in severe retribution for him.

The slave's problem was a question of obedience. The slave didn't obey his master, but he decided himself what he should do for his master. We act the same way in the church. We act and think according to how we feel God would react to us and our situations, instead of obeying Him by obeying His Word. Because we're under God's grace, His unmerited favor and blessings, are we free to sin? Of course not, and that's what Paul was saying to the people of the church in Romans. He went on to say, *"And having been set free from sin, you became slaves of righteousness." (Rom. 6:18) NKJV*. Let's obey our Master — Jesus Himself, who has great rewards awaiting us on that day. He's our Master who is perfect and true, unlike Satan, who is a liar.

We are slaves to whomever or whatever we obey, so why not be a slave to righteousness instead of a slave to sin? Being a slave to righteousness is actually experiencing freedom in Him for us, and not being enslaved or being dominated by sin but living freely and abundantly in Him. Live in the freedom purchased for us at Calvary's cross. *"In [this] freedom Christ has made us free [and completely liberated us]; stand fast then, and do not be hampered and held ensnared and submit again to a yoke of slavery [which you have once put off]." (Gal.5:1) AMP.* We are completely liberated to serve Him and those in church when we become slaves to His righteousness instead of being hampered and ensnared by the enemy. We have once put off the bondage of slavery, which oppresses, depresses, and withholds us from moving forward in His grace and truth, yet many in the church have submitted again to the yoke of slavery. *"And you shall know the truth, and the truth shall set you free." (Jn. 8:32) NKJV.*

Chapter 6

The Pharisaical Church

Sardis had been a capital of Lydia and was located about thirty miles southeast of Thyatira. The people's worship of the Roman Caesar and of Artemis, the goddess of fertility, was rampant in those days. It was a city of great wealth and fame. Perhaps the church was an image of the city itself — famous and rich. Perhaps it thrived like the city itself. It looked wonderful on the outside as the city itself did — healthy, prosperous, many people bustling about within its church walls. All seemed well, but it was far from well. Jesus stated in Rev. 3:1: *"I know your deeds; you have a reputation of being alive, but you are DEAD." (Italics mine. NIV).*

The Pharisaical Church

The church looked and felt vibrant and alive on the outside. It had a reputation to the outside world that it was a great and mighty church, but to Jesus it was spiritually lifeless; it was dead on the inside. He wasn't pleased at all. Why? What was going on in the church that Christ wasn't happy? He was aware of their deeds, whatever they were; they were known as being alive in the community, but He wasn't happy with their offering; their deeds were displeasing to Him, the only one we need to be concerned about pleasing. *"I have not found your deeds complete in the sight of my God." (Rev.3:2). NIV.*

Jesus said that the church's deeds weren't complete as He assessed and judged them. To be complete means to possess all of the necessary or appropriate parts. Synonyms for complete are perfect, absolute, full, whole, accomplish, and finish, just naming a few. The church lacked the necessary elements to make it complete and pleasing to God. Something was tragically missing within that church. It hadn't accomplished, finished, and perfected what God had intended for His church. Look at James 1:2-4: *"My brethren, count it all joy when you fall into various trials, knowing that the testing of your faith produces patience [endurance or perseverance]. But let patience have its perfect work, that you may be perfect [mature] and complete, lacking nothing." NKJV.* Verse 4 of the Amplified Bible reads as follows: *"But let endurance and steadfastness and patience have full play and do a thorough work, so that you may be [people] perfectly and fully developed [with no defects], lacking in nothing."*

Perhaps Jesus was saying that they weren't complete because they experienced no trials, no persecution from the outside because they were just like the world; they weren't different. Their deeds and works were evident, but they weren't complete. They appeared spiritually alive and acceptable in their community, but the sins of the world, the lack of a moral compass, the conviction of His Word wasn't changing the community, but the community was changing the church!

The church at Sardis arguably is an image of the church in America today — it is spiritually dead! *"If they persecute me, they will persecute you also. If they obeyed my teaching, they will obey yours also. They will treat you this way because of my name, for they do not know the One who sent me." (Jn. 15:20B-21) NIV.*

Because Christians are not to be of the world, then persecution is inevitable, but the church then wasn't and the church now isn't being persecuted because it wasn't and isn't preaching the truth as it needs to be preached. If their deeds were complete then persecution would have come, but the church in Sardis perhaps had become just like the pagan society — the stench of sin — that surrounded it.

Instead of preaching the truth and standing by God, they compromised their values: His Word for their mere temporary fulfillment; their desires, their acceptance of sin instead of acceptance of God; the desire for money instead of a desire for God, because of the city's wealth and status. All this, despite Christ's promise of blessing when He said, *"Blessed are you when people insult you, and persecute you and falsely say all kinds of evil against you because of me. Rejoice and be glad, because great is your reward in heaven" (Matt.5:11-12) NIV.* They rejected His eternal and lasting promises for the promises and fulfillment of the moment, the temporary pleasures of life that don't reap us reward in heaven, but rather the reward of the other unbelievers and pagans in the world: an eternity in hell, separated from Jesus!

Sin crept into the church instead of Christ, and Jesus wasn't happy. He warned them to *"Wake up! Strengthen what remains and is about to die, for I have not found your deeds complete in the sight of my God. Remember, therefore, what you have received and heard; obey it and repent." (Rev.3:2-3A) NIV.* Jesus tells them to awake because they are dead, and to strengthen what remains. Otherwise it will die. There is a remnant within the church that exists today that isn't defiled or stained with the sin of the world that remains within our church walls. However, that remnant is dying too because of a failure within the church body as a whole to recognize their sins and to repent!

Sin within the church infiltrates the entire body and kills it. That's why we need to heed the warnings of Jesus when He warns the church to obey and repent. Otherwise He says later that He will come like a thief, and that we will not know at what time He will come to us. But sadly, there are those who won't listen today to His call, to heed His warning while we still have time.

The church at Sardis reminds us of what Paul said in 2 Timothy 3:5, when he talked about godlessness being rampant in the last days — and we are in the last days. He describes those in the church as having a form of godliness, but denying its power. They have a form of godliness on the outside, but they are dead on the inside, they have no power to fight the good fight of faith to resist the wiles of the enemy, because the power of Christ, the Holy Spirit, is non-existent within them to fight it.

The church in America in a large way has become just like the teachers of the law and the Pharisees in Jesus' day. They were religious men who appeared whole and full of life on the outside, but their hearts were far from Him. He accused them of being *"like whitewashed tombs, which look beautiful on the outside, but on the inside are full of dead men's bones and everything unclean. In the same way, on the outside you appear to people as righteous but on the inside you are full of hypocrisy and wickedness."* *(Matt.23:27-28) NIV.* Wow! What a condemnation from the Lord Himself!

These self-righteous men who thought they had everything right felt it was their right to judge and criticize others because they were better than everyone else and all was so well with them! Do you know people like that in the church today? Do they point fingers in their self-righteous attitudes at those they don't approve of? What is he doing here? Didn't he just get out of jail the other day? Who's this lady with the three kids and she's not married?

This woman sitting next to me reeks and is filthy. Their kids are too noisy and don't listen. Why don't they go to another church? Did you see that girl with the nose ring and tattoos and that boy with a Mohawk? They don't belong here with people like us. Those who judge others because of their past sins or present appearances have Pharisaical hearts! They come to church dressed in their Sunday best, willing to help anyone in need as long as they look like them, live like them, and produce a benefit to them. They appear to be good Christians in their appearance and sometimes in deeds, but they're not any better than the heathen, non-believing society, when they cast aspersions on those who don't dress like they do, worship like they do, and who haven't experienced the hardships in their lives like they have. They feel they have earned the right and authority to judge and ridicule them, just like the Pharisees did. They are nothing more than hypocrites, pointing the finger of venom and hate and judgment upon others because they feel they're worthy enough to do so. Those same people are filling our church pews every Sunday in the name of Jesus Christ!

Chapter 7

The Church of Dry Bones

The church in America is full of dry bones — bones that are dead among a vicious wasteland of sin. The cancer of sin will render our very bones lifeless and that's exactly what is happening today. Sin will dry up and decay our bones, rendering them useless for His kingdom. We then become spiritually dead. Even if the breath of God is within us, our bones will still be dry unless the Holy Spirit revives and awakens us again to the sin in our lives and we repent as a people and begin to live again and speak His truth.

In the book of Ezekiel, the prophet had a vision as he was transported to a valley of dry, lifeless, and bleached bones. He began to survey them as he passed all around them and saw that they were very dry. The Lord then asked him if he thought that those bones would live, but Ezekiel, being unsure, had to defer to God Himself in His infinite wisdom, because only He would know. God commanded Ezekiel to speak to the bones and command them to HEAR the Word of God. Miraculously, the bones began to come together, as did their flesh and sinews, but no life had yet to enter into them.

The army of bones needed the breath of God to come into them to live. When God's breath breathed into them, they stood upon their feet like a great army, but God said that these people said, *"Our bones are dry, our hope is lost, and we ourselves are cut off." (Ezk.37:11b) NKJV*. But the Lord put His Spirit into them that they should live and give glory to Him. Many in the church are just like that exceedingly great army, an army that looks mighty, strong, and powerful on the outside. The numbers are there. They are living, breathing souls, but they are dead on the inside, like dry and powerless bones because there is one thing missing — the indwelling of the Holy Spirit required to give them life and direction, to convict them of their sins that would lead to repentance! *"I will put My Spirit in you, and you shall live." (Ezek. 37:14A) NKJV.* If the Holy Spirit isn't evidenced in our lives within the church body, then we're effectively dead, not able to decipher sin from truth, light from darkness. We are hopelessly left to our own devices, utterly at the disposal of Satan to wreak the havoc in our lives that he has done and continues to do right inside the walls of the church, as families are disintegrating, marriages are lost, children are committing suicide and engaging in illicit drugs, and pornography is rampant.

When God breathed the breath of life into the great army in Ezekiel, it was the same breath he breathed into Adam when he created him. Genesis 2:7 says, *"And the Lord God formed man out of the dust of the ground, and BREATHED into his nostrils the BREATH of life, and he became a living being."*

NKJV. He created within Adam what He created within us — the human spirit capable of moral, intellectual, and spiritual capabilities.

Man was made perfect until SIN entered into the equation. When sin entered the human race through Adam and Eve, we became spiritually dead, *"our bones dry, our hope lost."* We needed someone to save us from our guaranteed destination — HELL, a place where we'll be separated from God for all eternity.

Jesus entered into the picture and offered Himself as a sacrifice; He died so we didn't have to, even though we deserved it. He became sin for us, as is stated in 2 Corinthians 5:21, *"For God made Christ, who never sinned, to be the offering for our sin, so that we could be made right with God through Christ." NLT*. It is through His sacrificial death that we are set free, free from eternal damnation.

It's not enough that we're given the very breath of God to experience the physical life we now have, as the great army realized. They and we need something more. We need the Holy Spirit to give us that true life, the energized life that we need and desire, a life that recognizes that we have hope in Jesus Christ, that all is not lost! But the church in America is full of dry bones! Oh yes! We are living, breathing, individual people, given the breath of life by God, but that doesn't mean that we're saved, that we're delivered from the sin that *"so easily entangles."*

Isn't that what the people in church feel today? They come to church; they pay their tithes; they teach Sunday school, sing or play on the worship team, or they are even pastors who preach every Sunday. I have life! God has given me life, right? True, He has given us life. *"I have come that they may have life, and have it to the full." John10:10. NIV.* But what does He mean by that? Jesus said that He has come that we might have life, but is it the life HE desires AND requires of us?

That life He describes is a life given to Him and for Him, not for us. It's the quality of life we experience when our sin is sacrificed at His altar, and a new life created within us for His glory and purposes. It's a life of salvation, a life of sustenance; a life lived in service to Him, a life willing to be laid down or sacrificed for Him and His purposes and not ours. However, we're so consumed with sin and our own fleshly desires that we can't even hear from Him. We don't know what He means when He says He has come so we may experience that abundant life. We inject ourselves into the conversation and begin to tell God what Jesus meant when He spoke about the abundant life He offers us.

However, sin refuses to hear from God! Our self-indulgent need puts ourselves first, our own fleshly needs and desires first, it puts *us* on the throne of our life and not God. Our self-indulgent needs cry out to Him in anger and our fists shake at God, telling Him to stay out of our lives, to leave us alone. We know what's best and He doesn't. "I know, God that it's fine to live with my boyfriend or girlfriend before I'm married." "Your Word doesn't apply to me today,

God." "Everyone else is doing it in the church, so why can't I? Even the pastor doesn't speak out against it!"

Sin teaches that we fulfill our desires any way we want to fulfill them outside of God's wisdom and guidance. However, Jesus' abundant life teaches that sin, our self-indulgent desires, must go. His life taught us that to live a life pleasing to Him and a life that gives us fulfillment here and in eternity requires that He is on the throne, that He calls the daily shots in our lives, and not us.

Just like the Spirit was placed into the army of dry bones, He wants to place the Holy Spirit within us! The Holy Spirit wasn't BREATHED into them; the Holy Spirit was PLACED within them. We already have breath; we already have life, but that doesn't mean that they add up to eternity with Him! When we come to Him with our lives, He places the Spirit within us and we THEN, and only THEN, begin to live! And then He also promises that when we receive the Holy Spirit that we *"shall know that I, the Lord, have spoken and performed it," says the Lord. Ezek.*

37:14B NKJV. What an awesome promise of God, that we SHALL know, not MAY know, that He has spoken AND performed the act of placing the Holy Spirit within us.

Chapter 8

The Work of the Holy Spirit is Missing

The Holy Spirit, the Third Person of the Trinity, was given to us as a deposit, a down payment if you will, as His (Jesus') seal or pledge given to us when He went back to the Father in heaven after His resurrection. *"And he (God) has identified us as His own by PLACING the Holy Spirit in our hearts as the first installment that guarantees everything He has promised us." 2 Cor. 1:22 NLT*. The Holy Spirit is to reign within the hearts of believers within His church, leading, guiding, and directing us into all truth, but we've allowed that truth to be usurped by the enemy, who is the father of all lies and who has no truth within him. Yes, rather than being guided by the Holy Spirit within the church, we are guided by Satan, doing his bidding instead of following the Holy Spirit!

Jesus stated this in John 16:7-11: *"Nevertheless, I tell you the truth; it is to your advantage that I go away, for if I do not go away, the Helper (Holy Spirit) will not come to you. But if I go, I will send Him to you."* Jesus tells us the role the Holy Spirit will fulfill when we let Him do what He was sent to do in our lives. Jesus continues, *"And when He comes, He will convict the world concerning sin, righteousness and judgment."* These are three of the areas where the Holy Spirit will convict us. He convicts and doesn't condemn, because those who are in Christ Jesus are convicted when we sin by the Holy Spirit, not condemned. Romans 8:1 teaches that, *"Therefore there is now no condemnation for those who are in Christ Jesus." NIV.* Jesus said the Holy Spirit will come to convict those in sin when He continues with His words in John, *"concerning sin because they do not believe in me."* Yes, there are those within the church who call themselves born again and claim to be washed clean by the blood of Jesus shed for them, who openly weep during the time of worship and yet truly don't believe in Him because their sin-plagued lives were not left at the cross of Jesus, who will truly forgive when we come to Him with repentant hearts!

The other reason Jesus sent the Holy Spirit was to convict the world of righteousness. He continues this verse by stating, "Concerning righteousness because I go to the Father, and you will see Me no longer." Righteousness or justification before God is only found in Him, found in the persons of God the Father, the Son, and the Holy Spirit. The Holy Spirit that Jesus sent to us leads us into righteous lives lived only through Him and for Him. Apart from Him, there is no one righteous or anyone able to attain that righteousness on their own. Romans 3:10 states, *As it is written: There is no one righteous — not even one." NIV.*

We have people in the church, and even pastors, living the lives that they desire and assume to be righteous, when in fact they're not! Jesus' death on the cross was the righteous payment that pleased God and allowed us to experience the righteousness found in Christ. The Holy Spirit convicts us of our need for righteousness in this life as He strengthens us to help us lead the righteous life that He desires, despite the fact we live in the world, and especially when America's desire is to turn away from Him, wrongfully thinking that man's laws are more important than God's laws! Wow, what judgment is coming to those who think they have righteousness in and through themselves!

That leads us to the next point: judgment. The Holy Spirit will convict the world of judgment because Satan will finally be judged and the Holy Spirit's job is to remind us of that judgment to come. But if the Holy Spirit isn't reigning in the hearts of believers, they will be judged alongside the devil! He continues to try to convict those in the church every day. Yes, you may rightly state that He is talking about the world, and He is, but the world has come into the church, a very welcome visitor on a weekly and sometimes daily basis, and has thus blinded the people to the truth of God's Word available through the Holy Spirit.

It's sad and equally frightening to realize that those inside the church will be judged alongside the devil! This is not what God desires, as He *"wants everyone to be saved and understand the truth." (1 Tim. 2:4) NLT*. It's also stated in 2 Peter 3:9 that God does *"not want anyone to perish, but everyone to come to repentance." NIV*.

His desire is that we repent and be saved, which in turn allows us to understand the truth: God the Father, God the Son, and God the Holy Spirit. However, as stated earlier, sin's desire is for us and it wants to control our very live. Jesus desires that we have life and have it in abundance, but Satan's desire is to steal, kill, and destroy, yet we allow him to do it every day in our lives through our sinful deeds and thoughts that are far from God's heart, far away from a repentant heart that will save us.

"God didn't send His Son into the world to condemn it, but that the world through Him might be saved." Jn. 3:17. NKJV. When Jesus comes again, though, He's coming in judgment against those who refused His offer of salvation. Yes, there will be people who are in church every week, including pastors, who will face judgment when Christ returns! That Scripture goes on to state those who already believe aren't condemned, but saved for eternity with Him, but those who refuse to believe are already condemned because they don't believe in the name of Jesus Himself.

Jesus goes on to explain what that condemnation is when he continues in John 3:19, *"And this is the condemnation, that the light (Jesus) has come into the world, and men loved darkness rather than the light, because their deeds were evil." NKJV.* Jesus' reason for judgment was the condemnation of man because of their sin. When people love darkness, serving Satan rather than the light, Jesus, they will be condemned! That's God's judgment coming upon mankind for their sin-infested lives.

How can the Holy Spirit be our Helper as Jesus intended if, due to our sin, we reject Him and His guidance? The Holy Spirit was sent to help us in our everyday walk. Jesus promised His disciples and us that before He ascended to heaven, He would send the Holy Spirit when He said, *"But the Helper, the Holy Spirit, whom the Father will send in my name, he will teach you all things and bring to your remembrance all that I have said to you." Jn. 14:26. NIV.*

We cannot receive what we don't want. How can the Holy Spirit teach us all things and help to bring to remembrance what Jesus has taught us if we don't receive what the Father intends to send us? The answer is simple — we can't. That's why we walk around aimlessly, without guidance, or wisdom, or power, or purpose because we don't know the teachings of Jesus. The Holy Spirit isn't within us, calling to remembrance those things we need to empower us against the enemy, and we wonder why our lives are in disarray.

Chapter 9

The Church is Defenseless

When we live in this sinful world without Jesus' guidance through the Holy Spirit, we leave ourselves completely defenseless against the enemy's schemes. We are like soldiers who are going into war totally without armor, without any defense shield to protect us from the enemy. Would a soldier go into battle defenseless, without his or her weapons of warfare? Of course not, but we do it every day. We go into battle each day unarmed, not ready to battle the enemy, or we go into battle with the weapons of this world like anger-filled or vengeful words, bitterness, wrath, unforgiveness, and other weapons that aren't pleasing to God because

The Church is Defenseless

we believe these are the appropriate weapons to fight our daily battles. We truly do not believe that we have all we need in Him to wage our battles, thus not using them at all or not appropriately utilizing them.

We, the church, have all we need to send the enemy scurrying for his life, out of the battlefield we call life, but through unbelief, SIN, we allow him to remain to "steal, kill, and destroy" us! Paul, speaking to the church at Ephesus, instructed the Ephesian church and us in Ephesians 6:11 when he said, *"Put on the whole armor {the armor of a heavy-armed soldier which God supplies}, that you may be able to successfully to stand up against {all} the strategies and the deceits of the devil." AMP*.

Paul instructed we clothe ourselves with the WHOLE armor of God, and not just armor, but the whole, appropriate armor, because we can't go into battle half-armed; we leave ourselves exposed to the enemy on the battlefield. Enemies rejoice when they witness someone not fully armed for battle. Let us take a brief look at what the armor is that he's referring to, because Paul was speaking to the people IN church. Not the unsaved, but the saved!

First, Paul states in V.10 that we need to be strong in the Lord and His mighty power. Our strength is only in Him and not of ourselves. When we go to battle against the enemy, it is Christ who infuses us with the power and strength to wage our battle; our strength is found in our personal relationship with Him. The Amplified Bible talks about us being *"empowered through our union with Him."* V.10.

Second, Paul rightly mentions that our fight is not against each other, flesh and blood (physical opponents), but against the world rulers of this present darkness, whom the Amplified Bible portrays as *"the master spirits"* of this world, and it's also against the spirit forces of wickedness in the heavenly or supernatural sphere. We need to know this within the church. Our battles in this life are not against each other, despite what we may read or hear portrayed in the media on a daily basis. Our battle isn't against atheists, agnostics or anyone else, except those demonic spirits working through them. It's not a war against religions, as some believe it to be, or even a race war, but a war against the rulers or despots in this sinful world and the many legions of Satan's army in the heavenlies. Once we know against whom we are fighting, then we can appropriately arm ourselves to do battle, but we can't wage war against an opponent we don't know or against the wrong opponent, therefore wasting our much-needed resources of time and energy fighting the wrong battle. And wrong opponent.

Once we know who our opponent or enemy is, we're ready to wage an effective war against them. We then prepare to wage the appropriate war. As stated earlier, we need to prepare ourselves fully by wearing the full armor of God afforded us. Why would we want to engage in a war by using the elements of the world that the enemy already employs to wage our battle? He has already tried that and has failed miserably. Remember the work of Jesus upon the cross? Remember His death and ultimate resurrection, thereby defeating death? Satan already donned and employed his battle gear and failed miserably! Christ defeated him! No matter what he threw at Jesus, it was feeble and failed miserably. These same strategies, if you will, that Jesus used to defeat the enemy are available to us today, so why would we want to wage our battle, or re-invent the wheel with our own defenses that are weak and feeble, without power, when Jesus has already been battle-tested, fought the fight, and defeated Satan? It doesn't make sense, but if we're not MENTALLY prepared to do battle, or if we don't believe in the strategies already deployed and successful, we lose the battle before we even start. We are weak, not prepared for battle, and the enemy knows it. Let's be prepared with what God instructs us to wear and we'll be successful every time!

The devil deploys deceitful and subtle weapons of warfare to defeat us. Paul spoke to the Corinthian church about his concern for them as their spiritual mentor, and didn't want them to be deceived as he presented those within the church as a chaste virgin betrothed to one husband — Christ. We should take heed to listen to his God-given word when in 2 Corinthians 11:3 he stated, *"But I fear, lest somehow, as the serpent deceived Eve by his craftiness, so your minds may be corrupted from the simplicity that is in Christ." (NKJV).*

The devil is deceitful and deception is his master plan that he deploys against us within the church. As Eve fell for it in the garden, therefore allowing sin into the world and forever changing it, those within the church are falling for that same deception because of their own sin! They've allowed Satan entry into their minds to wreak havoc; all because we're not armed with the whole armor of God!

The Amplified Bible states that we need to guard against being *"corrupted and seduced from wholehearted and sincere and pure devotion to Christ."* That pure devotion is undefiled, unadulterated, and sinless devotion to Christ. We are devoted to Him and not the enemy. It's that pure child-like faith that's not corrupted. As Paul was concerned with the

Corinthian church, God is concerned with the church in America, and He's VERY concerned.

We have allowed the devil entry into our battlefield; the enemy has infiltrated the church through God's chosen people and they don't even know it. We then must ask if we'll be able to stand against the deceitfulness of the enemy without being prepared with the whole armor of God. The answer is that we can't and won't. Paul continues in Ephesians 6:13 by saying that we *"may be able to withstand in the evil day, and having done all, to stand."* Every day is an evil day where the enemy is concerned because his very existence is consumed by attempting to *"steal, kill, and destroy"* God's people. However, we're easy pickings if we're not prepared. We need to employ all that God has given us so we could stand, which means to be immovable, strong, and powerful. Once the enemy deploys his weapons of warfare and realizes we're ready to do battle, he has no chance. He must flee and the battle has been won. We have withstood his tactics and stood firm.

Chapter 10

Where are Our Weapons of Warfare?

*I*f we're going to battle with His whole armor, what is it that we must wear for battle? Paul continues in Chapter 6 of Ephesians where he mentions to *"gird your waist with truth."* Soldiers in ancient times would gird themselves with a belt that had strips of leather that hung below the waist to protect them when they were in battle. We must gird ourselves with His truth. God desires honest, truth-speaking people, and Jesus is the truth when He said, *"You shall know the truth and the truth shall set you free."* Jn. 8:32 NKJV. He further said,

"I am the Way, the Truth, and the Life. No one comes to the Father but by me." Jn. 14:6 NKJV.

He then states that we need to wear the breastplate of righteousness. The soldier's breastplate went completely around his waist, which also protected his back. It was made of leather and metal. We all have righteousness IN Christ, but Paul was also talking about our righteous character and deeds. If we speak the truth and have the truth in our lives, our character will be righteous, as will our deeds.

The Christian is then to have his feet shod with the gospel of peace. The soldier wore shoes that were studded and firm. We are to prepare ourselves for the spreading of the gospel, to be busy about God's business because the Gospel is true and firm.

Paul then states above all to carry with us the shield of faith: faith in our Lord and Savior Jesus Christ. The shield is to be used against everything Satan throws at us. The shield of faith stops all that the enemy can muster to throw at us. The Roman soldier used his shield to protect his whole armor. His shield generally measured two-and-a-half feet by four feet and any fiery darts thrown by the enemy couldn't penetrate his armor or shield. The same goes for us too. *"Without faith it is impossible to please God." Heb. 11:6 NIV.* God is pleased when we trust in Him to do the battle for us because He knows we'll be victorious and avoid many unnecessary heartaches, defeats, and disappointments in the battlefield of life that we suffer every day.

The next piece of armor we put on is the helmet of salvation. The helmet protected the soldiers' heads and made them look taller and more impressive than they were. When we're initially saved, don't we feel on top of the world, like we can conquer anything that comes our way? We feel great; we have Jesus on our side and we want to tell anyone who will listen about what Jesus did for us and what He could do for them. We express that child-like faith that has no worries or fears, but total faith and trust in God. We have that hot, burning fire of the Holy Spirit within us, who is ready to do battle for us because we stoke

Him on a daily basis because we wear the armor of God. But then ever so slowly, that fire begins to die out. It slowly burns to an ember within us, the passion and desire to serve Jesus begins to wane, and we leave ourselves vulnerable to the enemy, and he knows it.

Why does that fire slowly die? What has happened to the passion that we had when we were saved? Why does serving the Almighty God, the creator of heaven and earth, who loves us so much that He sent His one and only Son to die, become something we don't enjoy anymore, perhaps even become boring to do? It is purely and simply sin. Our self-indulgent needs begin to take over and the passion and fire of the Holy Spirit ebbs and we become our own master, people who go to battle unarmed. The fiery darts of the enemy are penetrating our very lives because the fire that had been burning within us isn't there anymore to easily quench the darts of the enemy. And we wonder why we, within the church, are so hurt and wounded? We are losing the battle because we've taken off the armor of God and have dressed ourselves with worldly, carnal battle gear that have no chance of defeating Satan and his minions. We need that fire burning again, that white hot fire of passion of the Holy Spirit, who appropriately arms us to quench those darts.

Finally, Paul tells us to take up the sword of the Spirit, which is the Word of God. It's the only offensive weapon mentioned and the only one we need to slay Satan in his tracks. It's the Word of God that sends him fleeing. He can't and won't ever successfully come against the Word of God when it is known and spoken. Scripture teaches in Isaiah 55:11, *"So shall my word be that goeth forth out of my mouth: it shall not return unto me void, but it shall accomplish that which I please, and it shall prosper in the thing whereto I sent it." KJV.* Paul was speaking about a specific Word that we speak forth, depending upon the battle we are waging, but we need to know His Word to speak it into that specific battle if we are to be successful because His Word is powerful and true.

Because He sends it through us, it will always prevail in the battlefield of life.

Isaiah talked about God's Word not returning to Him void, but that it will accomplish what the Lord pleases. The NLT (New Living Translation) states that God "*sends it out and it always produces fruit… and it will prosper everywhere I send it.*" Wow! His spoken Word always produces fruit that's pleasing to Him. It will always prosper wherever He sends it! That is so powerful and exciting!

Speak His Word; let it do its work, because He promises it will never return void, that His Word will accomplish whatever it needs to accomplish according to our specific need or battle. However, the key is to speak His Word. We need to spend time with Him; we need to study and meditate on His Word so we're fully prepared to answer the enemy.

Jesus gave us a perfect example of this in Luke 4 when He spent forty days and nights in the desert after having been baptized by John and before He began His public ministry. Satan thought it an opportune time to attack our Lord as he felt Him to be vulnerable, to be weakened after spending the time He did in the desert. Three different times he challenged our Lord, and three different times he failed. He tried to get Jesus to perform a miracle before his eyes, and then tried to get Him to worship him, and finally he even tried to twist the Word of God and to use it against Jesus. But what happened? Did Satan succeed? The Lord was vulnerable, right?

Satan did not succeed and Jesus was not vulnerable. Yes, He was hungry. And yes, He was weak, but weak physically, not spiritually. If you look at the first verse in Chapter 4, He was FILLED with the Holy Spirit. He was already empowered, spiritually speaking; He had the Word of God within Him that He spoke forth that stopped any and all fiery darts Satan threw at Him! He spoke the Word of God in every situation. It produced the fruit; the Word prospered and Satan couldn't do anything about it but flee.

If we don't know the Word of God, Satan will also twist the Word to make us doubt, to question

God's truth and goodness. If we know it, however, he is no match for us. Jesus was ready. He was filled with the Holy Spirit, and He had God's Word within Him. We'll suffer physically, but that doesn't have to affect us spiritually. Unfortunately, sadly, it does, and it does all too often.

The fire of the Holy Spirit must be burning brightly. Luke doesn't mention that Jesus was lacking. He wasn't. He didn't say that Jesus was partially filled with the Spirit, but that He was FILLED with the Spirit. He lacked nothing. And then He spoke the Word. We need to do the same thing. Keep the fire burning brightly and speak His Word, and have the sword of the Spirit with you and be ready to do battle.

Satan will also use any tactic of deception that he can, as he even tried to use the Word against Jesus. People will try to use Scripture to twist it to suit their own needs and desires and believe they are speaking God's will, because they are using the Word. Upon closer look, though, Satan didn't fully use the Word of God, as he left out a crucial phrase when he tested Jesus. When Satan quoted Psalm 91 and verses 11 and 12, he purposely left out the phrase, *"to keep you in all your ways."* God will keep us and protect us in all our ways, not just some of the time but all of the time.

But Satan has deluded those within the church to believe that God has not and will not protect them. They are following Satan's tactics and deception. As stated earlier they'll misuse or misquote Scripture, and only use certain parts of it to suit their needs, and it's sinful. We don't want the full truth of the Gospel, the truth that will set us free from our fleshly, carnal thoughts and deeds, and give us a full desire to serve Him and Him alone, despite the persecution from the world.

Jesus was persecuted by Satan, the Sadducees and Pharisees, and even from His own people. They rejected Him because the truth was in Him, but they didn't desire the truth because it didn't mesh with His desire for them- a true and eternal personal relationship with Him. They wanted things done their own way without His guidance, but Jesus forged ahead. He accomplished what He came to do — to suffer and die for the sins of the people!

Jesus didn't allow the enemy to thwart what He was assigned to do. He had a purpose and plan of God to fulfill, as those in the church have as well. Yes, the persecution was brutal, but He had a close, intimate relationship with God and wouldn't allow the devil to deter Him from what He was chosen to do. He was filled with the Holy Spirit; He walked in the power of the Holy Spirit. He stayed connected to His source; He knew the Word, as He was the Word and spoke it forth and it was powerful. *"For the word of God is alive. Sharper than any two-edged sword; it penetrates even to dividing soul and spirit, joints and marrow; it judges the thoughts and attitudes of the heart." Heb. 4:12. NIV.*

Jesus believed that the Word of God was alive and active, and yes, it is even alive today! It is powerful when spoken forth in all its fullness and power, and the enemy has no chance. No circumstance, trial, or persecution you may be facing in church today is too difficult to overcome when the Word of God is employed to do battle for us. It is sharper than any two-edged sword. The two-edged sword was used for thrusting and piercing the enemy, but God's Word is even stronger than the most powerful, earthly tool. It penetrates our very being, even judging the thoughts and attitudes of our heart.

Chapter 11

Friendship with the World or God?

The church today refuses to have the Word of God judge our hearts, attitudes, and thoughts, because the darkness within will be brought to the light and judged. We never want to leave our sins exposed because we won't like what God sees, like He doesn't know already! We all look good on the outside. We portray to the church body and the world that, "All is okay because I'm a child of God," when, in fact, all is not okay and God wants to do a work in us like He's never done before! Who cares what other people think or what they might say? We should only be concerned what our righteous and true Judge has to say about the sin in our lives. *"We all have sinned and fall short of the glory of God." Rom. 6:23 NIV.* We're all sinners in need of God's grace, but it's the sin that we're living in, that we don't want to stop committing because it feels good or we're deluded into thinking it's not sin. Or we think that because God does know the intentions of my heart, if I mean well, He will forgive me.

Satan is the great deceiver and he will trick you into thinking God isn't just, or that God wouldn't punish us because He's too good! Too many in the church believe that because they're saved that they can do anything they want because God is a merciful and forgiving God. They think that everything is going to be fine. But that is simply a lie from the pit of hell because God is a forgiving and merciful God, but He's also a righteous and just God who must punish sin.

He cannot and will not turn a blind eye to sin, as many pastors do in the church today. He will judge sin because He is a just God! We will not escape His judgment. *"The judgments of the Lord are true and righteous altogether." Ps. 19:9.* However, right before those words, Psalm 19 states that His law is perfect, converting the soul. His Word, the Scripture, is perfect and converts the soul, converts those living in darkness, separated from Him for eternity, to His marvelous light, a future with Him for all eternity.

His Holy Word needs to be taught in the church today, but it's not because it has watered down, twisted, and conformed to the liking of the congregation because the members demand it. Pastors begin to pay heed to church attendance, the tithes and offerings being deposited in the collection plate every week. The board doesn't like the conviction of sin being preached, so they demand that the pastor change his message, and he does. Instead of searching God's heart, they listen to the hearts of the people and there's no fear of God. There's no fear of the sin that's rampant in the church. The church then succumbs to the bidding of the devil instead of submitting before God.

"All Scripture is God-breathed (given by His inspiration) and profitable for instruction, for reproof

and conviction of sin, for correction in error and discipline in obedience, [and] for training in righteousness (in holy living, in conformity to God's will in thought, purpose, and action). 2 Tim.3:16. AMP. There is much value in God's Word as it is profitable for our well-being. It trains us to live a righteous life, rebukes us, corrects us, disciplines us, and yes, even convicts us of our sin! But how could we be convicted of our sin when His Word isn't being taught correctly, if it's watered down to fit the needs of those "itching ears"?

There is no profit in His Word if the people aren't taught to live by it. Regarding the lack of profitability living by the world's standards, Jesus taught us in Matthew 16:26, *"For what profit is it to a man if he gains the whole world and loses his own soul?" NKJV*. Jesus was referring to whether or not we, the church, would serve Him or serve the world, which is Satan's playground or domain. Many in the church are sacrificing their very salvation because they're not *"taking their cross and following Him"* because it's too hard, they say, too difficult a path to walk because of the persecution we face. It's just simply easier living the way we want to live in this world, wrongly and deceitfully believing God will understand.

Yet God states in James very clearly, *"Do you not know that friendship with world is enmity with God? Whoever therefore wants to be a friend of the world is an enemy of God." NKJV*. James spoke about believers who were spiritual adulterers and adulteresses. The Amplified Bible talks about those in the church being like unfaithful wives who are having illicit or sinful love affairs with the world, who then break their marriage vow to God!

James was referring to those in the church who fight about worldly or materialistic things instead of concerning themselves with the things of God, and that's what the church in America is like today! Sin has crept in, as we want our self-indulgent (sin) needs satisfied over a deeper, more intimate relationship with Jesus Christ. James had said that those within the church were quarreling, fighting, lusting, coveting, and even committing murder! He said their prayers were for their own sinful desires instead of God's desire for their lives, and it's the same today, except that it's a spreading cancer that's going to destroy the church unless it's dealt with.

Having a friendship or relationship with the world will not get us any closer to God, but it will only drive us further away from Him and His covenant protection of us because we have broken our covenant with Him by bringing the world into the church.

Sin is an accepted practice in the world and we have become desensitized to it. It is habitual and will destroy us, so it has no place in the church today. The Scripture will not become profitable unless it convicts us of the sin we're living in today. Unless we become a God-centered church and not an I-centered church, it will never be a church pleasing to God. It says we become His enemy, and we know what happens to enemies. They're destroyed. Don't we want to please God and restore our covenant relationship with Him rather than become His enemy, whom He will judge? He will restore us in His infinite goodness, but it's up to us to let Him to that.

Referring back to Psalm 19, it states that the Lord's testimony is sure, making the wise simple. God's testimony is true and it's living, making those who think they are wise simple. And what is His testimony? 1John 5:11 states this: *"And this is the testimony: That God has given us eternal life, and this life is in His Son." NKJV*. Eternal life is in Jesus Christ and the Scripture John wrote continues, *"Whoever has the Son has life; whoever does not have the Son of God does not have life." NIV*. Can this testimony be any simpler than that? Whoever has Jesus, meaning whoever has given their life over to Him, whoever has taken up their cross and follows Him daily has eternal life. It means more than saying the "Sinner's Prayer" of repentance. It's more than attending church every week, or teaching Sunday school or playing on the worship team or whatever it is you do in church. It's being so repulsed by sin that you repent of it and ask Christ to forgive you, to give you a fresh start and to do everything you can in your daily walk with Him to make your life a sweet-smelling aroma to Him, a life pleasing to Him.

Psalm 19 continues to say that God's statutes are right and bring the heart to rejoicing! David said earlier in this psalm that he did not put the Lord's statutes away from him. Leviticus 18:5 also states, *"I am the Lord your God. You shall therefore keep my statutes and judgments, which if a man does he shall live by them: I am the Lord." NKJV.* Of course, breaking the statutes in the Old Testament brought on death to that person, which resulted in Jesus Christ coming as the fulfillment of the Law, meaning we weren't bound by the law anymore but free in Christ.

David's psalm continues by saying that God's commandments were not only pure, meaning undefiled, not stained by sin, but perfect, and also enlightening to the eyes! His commandments should be honored and upheld so the sin in our lives would be eradicated and our eyes opened to the sin. *"And this is His commandment: that we should believe on the name of His Son Jesus Christ and love one another as He gave us commandment." 1 Jn. 3:23. NKJV.* Jesus Christ is our light and He provides the enlightenment to reveal the sins in our lives so He could wash them in His blood, but we must believe in Him by following Him.

David, in Psalm 18, also said that God is merciful to those who are merciful, and He will show Himself blameless to those who are blameless. Blameless is someone who has rightfully and humbly dealt with their sin openly and without shame. Jesus won't bring shame upon those who come to Him, because He will show mercy and blamelessness to those who come to Him.

After the commandment David talks about in Psalm 19, he continues to say in verse 9 that the fear of the Lord is clean, that it endures forever! Proverbs 1:7 says, *"The fear of the Lord is the beginning of knowledge, but fools {sinners} despise wisdom and instruction." NKJV.* The fear of the Lord discussed here isn't a spirit of fear, but a reverential, respectful fear of the Creator of the universe, God Almighty! We need to fear Him so much that we want to do all we can to please Him for FEAR of His righteous judgment.

The spirit of fear doesn't come from God but Satan. 2 Timothy 1:7 is clear on this. *"For God does not give us a spirit of fear, but of power, love, and of a sound mind (self-discipline)." NKJV.* This isn't a reverential fear but a fear or cowardice to do His work or to tell Satan to hit the road that we're not interested in our own self-indulgent needs where he tempts us to sin so we lose that connection we have with God. It's not the same reverential fear that we must have towards God, but a fear that keeps us from Him and with the enemy. Fear can be crippling and keep us in our sin and away from Christ's saving grace. This is not the spirit God has imparted to us.

It's clear that He imparts to us His love, power, and a sound mind and not a spirit of fear. These are imparted to us through the Holy Spirit within us, but it's up to us to allow them to be utilized as God intended them to be utilized. If so, what a powerful witness we make for the Lord.

Psalm 19 verse 9B continues with *"the judgments of the Lord are true and righteous altogether." NKJV*. Altogether means totally, complete, fully, wholly. God's judgments are complete, whole, and full. There's no room for error, we cannot change His judgments. They're already complete and whole. Something that is whole is complete, so God doesn't change His judgments, nor is He ever wrong. It's been said that, "God is not fair." That's true! He's not fair! He's just! *"Jesus Christ is the same yesterday and today forever." Heb. 13:8. NIV*. Jesus Christ is the same from eternity past, now, and forever. He will deal with sin because He must. He's righteous and true and that power belongs to Him.

David is informing us in this psalm that Scripture should be desired even more than gold, meaning wealth, material possessions or accumulations, verse

10. We should want to abide by His written Word no matter the cost, no matter the opportunity presented us that would fulfill our self-indulgent needs (sins). He further writes that if we keep them there is a reward for us, actually a great reward!

God will reward us for our faithfulness to Him by extending to us a seat at His banquet table in heaven. The Book of Life is written with a personal invitation on it for you and me! This is a promise from God to each one of us! It's a promise of eternity with Him in heaven, having a special seat at His table to commune and worship Him forever! What could be better than that?! However, those in the church don't see it, don't believe it, or simply don't care! They care more about their own needs being fulfilled rather than the needs of their neighbors and those in their community, and that's not what God desires for those of us in the church.

God's plans and purposes for those in the church are good, but we become impatient, and let the temptation of the world draw us away from those plans and promises. Jeremiah 29:11 states, *"For I know the plans I have for you," says the Lord. "They are plans for good and not disaster, to give you a future and a hope." NLT.* You see, God has PLANS for us, but His plans won't come to fruition unless we first deal with the sin in our lives. That's up to us, not Him. He plans good for us and not evil or disaster. He also plans to give us a future and a hope! Aren't these great plans He has for us? Who doesn't want good to happen to them? Who doesn't want to be given a good future and a hope? Good in this life and in the life to come? A future and hope with Him! Amen and amen!

He has promised us a great reward or good when we follow His Word, as evidenced in the psalm. He also then plans that future in heaven with Him and Jesus is our hope! However, plans don't come to fruition unless we follow God's way, unless we follow His plans, and not our plans. He alone determines what is good and what our hope and future are.

Chapter 12

Genesis of Sin

The sin in our lives robs us of the goodness God intends for us to receive. Sin robs us of our hope — Jesus Christ. Sin robs us of the future He desires for us, a future in eternity with Him. Sin robs us of every single thing God has planned for us, yet we keep sinning anyway, believing because we attend church that somehow shields us from God's impending judgment.

How have we become so deceived to believe that the sin we're committing will somehow be forgotten just because we attend church? This is simply a lie we've come to believe and need to look no further than the beginning for its genesis. It began with the beginning of the human race back in the book of Genesis. We need to look no further than the Garden of Eden, where sin befell the human race.

The Garden of Eden was created by God for all of us to enjoy forever. Man and woman were to dwell in perfect harmony with God for all eternity. Man knew no sin at this time. Sin hadn't entered the world. Adam and Eve knew no sin. They dwelled in perfect harmony with Him. He had PLANNED that it would be like this forever. Imagine having all of your needs met by God and not ourselves. Imagine having all of God's provision and to never be in want. That's what it was like in the Garden of Eden.

Eden was a place of eternal bliss. It's believed to be more closely related to an Aramaic root meaning "fruitful, well-watered." This place was perfect! God had planned for us to enjoy His perfect handiwork forever, but when we became involved, when we put our own needs and desires ahead of God's desires, we messed it up. What was perfect became imperfect.

God had placed there every tree known to man that was pleasant to the eyes and provided food. There was even a river that *"went out of Eden to water the garden." Gen. 2:10. NKJV.* There were four rivers coming out of the garden that formed four riverheads. There was gold and onyx and bdellium. Bdellium is an aromatic gum like myrrh that exudes from a tree. The garden was plentiful; it was beautiful. It fulfilled everything God had desired for man, but it still wasn't enough.

God had commanded Adam that he was free to eat from each and every tree in the garden, but not from the tree of the knowledge of good and evil. He even commanded that should he eat from it he would surely die. God's commands are always clear. He never leaves us to wonder if what He says is true or not. He never brings chaos and confusion. His commands and precepts are always true. *"For God is not a God of disorder but of peace — as in all the congregations of the Lord's people." 1 Cor. 14:33. NIV.* The King James Version states that God *"is not the author of confusion*." When He does speak, as He does in His Word, there's nothing to question; there's nothing that's ambiguous or confusing. He warned Adam and He was clear about what he should and shouldn't do.

Despite having instructions from God, we sin. We are sinners. We desire our own fleshly needs to be fulfilled in the way we want them fulfilled. There was a serpent in the garden (Satan) that Genesis 3 describes as being *"more cunning than any beast of the field which the Lord God had made." NKJV*. Satan immediately questioned God's judgment when he attacked Eve with his cunning words. He tempted her much like Jesus was tempted in the desert, but with much different results, of course!

Satan is deceptive and will always question God's Word, His judgment. He did this with Eve when he asked if she was not able to eat from any trees in the garden. Of course he knew this to not be true. Satan knows the Word, and he knows of God's commands. That's why we need to know His Word and know it well, because Satan will always use deception to tempt us to not trust God and His Word, and he will know when we don't know it. He'll know when we don't have a right relationship with Him. That's why we always need to be in the Word and prayer, so we're rightly prepared when the enemy comes at us, especially when we give him an opportune time to come at us as he did with Eve.

Satan had already realized that she had given him a foothold when she responded by telling him, incorrectly, that God had said that she and Adam were allowed to eat of every tree in the garden except from the tree of knowledge of good and evil, but she also said that they weren't allowed to TOUCH the tree, which God did not say — and Satan knew it!

Once we give Satan an open door, no matter how slightly we open that door, we give him a foothold, and we're in deep trouble. The propensity to sin increases dramatically because he realizes we're not in communion with God as we believe we are. That doesn't mean we'll sin, but the chances increase, and when they increase, if we're not fully prepared to speak His perfect Word in response to his deception, we'll sin every time.

Once Satan realizes our relationship with God could be in question, he ups the ante! He did so with Eve when he told her that she would not die if she ate of the tree. He blatantly and openly called God a liar! Even Jesus stated this in John chapter 8, when in verse 44 He was speaking to the Pharisees regarding Satan when He said, *"You are of your father the devil, and the desires of your father you want to do. He was a murderer from the beginning, and does not stand in the truth, because there is no truth in him. When he speaks a lie he speaks from his own resources, for he is a liar and the father of it." NKJV.*

Jesus says that Satan is the father of all lies, as it all started in him in the garden. There is no truth in him and never will be, yet we bow to him every day when we submit to his temptation to distrust God's truth found in Jesus Christ! Jesus proclaimed in John

14:6 that *"I am the way, the truth, and the life. No one comes to the Father except through Me." NKJV.*

Jesus described the Pharisees as a group of men who denied Jesus as the truth, as they were very antagonistic and hateful towards Him. Those who choose to follow their own means of self-salvation are followers of Satan. That's not harsh! That's truth! Jesus said so and there are many Pharisaical people filling up the pews in church every Sunday, condemning Jesus and His truth because no one wants to hear that they're living in sin.

Sin is either not talked about or replaced with words like mistakes, shortcomings, errors, etc., instead of calling it what it is. The minute we try to make excuses or not treat sin as seriously as it needs to be treated, the enemy knows it and comes in for the kill. The truth hurts and hurts deeply, but if we don't personally deal with the sins in our lives, we'll never fulfill what the Lord has for us in this life and beyond.

Prior to Jesus' scathing rebuke of the Pharisees He had asked why they didn't understand His speech, which was a rhetorical question of course because He knew the heart of man. He said they weren't able to understand His Word because His Truth wasn't abiding in them. If it was, they would have been followers of Him as we would be today. But when we choose to not follow Him by not living in His truth, we serve the devil; we do his bidding. Our desires then don't become God's desires for our lives, but the devil's desires for our lives. Jesus said so in His condemnation of the Pharisees. He said that they desired to serve Satan and were his followers.

Jesus also stated that Satan speaks from his own resources. He doesn't speak for God or anyone else. He speaks for himself and himself alone. Jesus then asks why, when He speaks the truth, we don't believe Him. Isn't He asking the same of the church in America today? Why is His truth usurped by the lies of the devil? It's because of the sin in our lives and our desires to serve our flesh, which in turn serves the devil. Who convicts us of sin? Jesus convicts us of sin, and He alone. Jesus convicts, but the devil condemns.

Jesus proceeded by saying that he who hears God's words are of God and those who don't hear aren't of God. When Jesus is talking about hearing His Word, He is talking about actually putting it into practice in our daily lives. People can say they hear, but unless they listen, unless they put those words they've heard into action, it doesn't mean anything. To hear Jesus is to listen to Him by putting His Words into action.

Eve didn't listen to God's spoken Word. He had told Adam and Eve to not eat of the tree of knowledge of good and evil. She didn't truly HEAR His Word, because she didn't put it into PRACTICE. That's the key: she heard, but didn't hear. If she truly heard, she would have told the devil to flee in the name of God. She would have truly put the Lord's Words into action. When we do that, the devil has no defense. He MUST flee. He can't and never, ever will succeed against God — EVER!

Eve didn't do that because she wasn't in perfect communion with God in that moment. The temptation was there and she fell victim to Satan because of her lack of relationship with God. When she heard his deceptive, tempting words, and allowed him entry into her thought-life, she was already defeated. She had no defense because Satan knew that she didn't truly hear from God, because she didn't say and do exactly what He had told her according to His Word.

We do the same thing with God. We twist God's Word and quote what we think to be Scripture as His truth or we quote something believed to be in Scripture and it's not. Satan knew that Eve was susceptible and weak to his schemes and deception, and he knows when we are too. The serpent continued in Genesis 3:4-5 when he said, *"You won't die!" the serpent said to the woman. "God knows that your eyes will be opened as soon as you eat it, and you will be like God, knowing both good and evil." NLT*.

Since Satan had already succeeded by gaining entry into her thought life, he appealed to her senses, her pride in knowing good and evil. He called God a liar and also continued to lie by saying that she would be LIKE God, that she would be on the same level of God! Man is incapable of discerning what is good, but only evil and Satan knew that and God knows that. There is nothing good within Satan because — think about this for a moment — if there was any good in him, then why would he tempt her to eat of the forbidden fruit? He wouldn't because there would be some good within him, but he is as incapable of discerning what is good as we are without Christ! There is no good within Satan and there is no good within us APART from God.

Satan is the epitome of evil because there is no good in him, and there's no good in him because he's not in God but only full of himself, who is full of evil. Man, in sin, only knows evil. Were Adam and Eve like God in that they were able to discern what was good and what was evil? NO! Romans

3:10 states that, *"As it is written: There is no one righteous, not even one." (NIV).* None of us, apart from God, is righteous; none of us is good; we're only evil. Jesus even stated in Mark 10:18, *"Why do you call me good?" Jesus asked. "Only God is truly good." (NLT).*

Satan deceived Eve into thinking that she would discern both good and evil, and thus sin entered into the world when she disobeyed God's command and ate of the forbidden fruit. Adam, her husband, who was supposed to be protecting his wife, allowed this to happen and is perhaps more guilty than Eve. He also ate of the forbidden fruit, and then tried to play the role of victim by blaming God for giving him Eve! *"The woman you gave to be with me — she gave me [fruit] from the tree, and I ate." Gen.3:12 (AMP).*

Rather than being a man and taking responsibility for his own failures and weaknesses, he blamed God for this tragedy. So we have the sin of commission and the sin of arguing and condemning God for our own man-made situation, a situation created by us, and not God! Then there's shame of God's created beauty — the human race. They sewed fig leaves together to hide their nakedness, for they were ashamed. They also expressed their fear of being seen by God because of their wrongdoing. Adam said, *"I heard the sound of you [walking] in the garden, and I was AFRAID because I was naked; and I hid myself." Gen. 3:10 (AMP).*

Then, of course, there was the sin of disobedience. They disobeyed God's Word, thus determining what they felt to be both good and evil without realizing that their very thoughts and actions were evil and not pleasing to God. Don't we do the very thing that Adam and Eve did in our everyday life? We decide what's good and evil based upon what we decide to be good and evil. Apart from God, we only know to do evil and not good because God only truly knows what is good. Man only knows evil.

God did state in Genesis 3:22, *"Now the man has become like one of us and has knowledge of what is good and what is bad. He must not be allowed to take fruit from the tree that gives life, eat it, and live forever." GNB.* Man did obtain the KNOWLEDGE of what was good and evil, but his actions are always evil. He may know the difference between good and evil, but he will always choose evil apart from God.

Once Adam and Eve donned their sin nature, they had broken their perfect relationship with God. It is kind of ironic that God would state that they had become like Them, the Trinity, when God knows no sin, but is perfect. He was being sarcastic, as if man knew and believed he equated himself with the God of the universe.

If man had become like anyone, it wasn't God, but Satan. Satan lied by stating that they would become like God. Of course man may think he is like God or is God, but man is anything but God. Their self-indulgent needs of pride and disobedience only equated them with Satan. Man had become like him and Satan, in his evilness, knew exactly what he was doing because he only knows evil.

Because man had, for the first time, sinned and destroyed his personal relationship with God, everything about him was sin and evil. God had to pronounce His judgment upon man for his sin and God did just that. He banned them from the garden where they were blessed and favored, where they were protected, loved, and in perfect union with God. He could have killed them in that moment and would have been perfectly justified in doing so, but in His mercy and love He didn't do that.

First He didn't permit them the ability to eat from the tree of life and live. They were sinners who disobeyed God and they and we deserved death. Their sin had to be dealt with swiftly. Because of their sin nature, they couldn't receive eternal life by eating from the tree. They had to be punished for their sin. They were then banned from participating in all that God had offered them in the garden, and exiled them from it.

God pronounced His righteous judgment upon the devil, Adam, and Eve. Man would have much pain and sorrow in this life and his life would become mortal. God was grieved and is grieved today because of our sin, the sin that exists in the church. As God longed to have His relationship restored with Adam and Eve, He longs to have our relationship restored with Him, and His relationship restored with those within the church.

Chapter 13

Do We View the World Through God's Lenses or Man's?

Man is a depraved individual because of sin that began in the garden, and we became weak, depraved, mortal; producing everything evil without restraint, ignorant beasts, and the list could go on and on. This is what the sin nature does to us: it separates us from God's eternal mercy and grace, and salvation. God still loved His children and didn't destroy them, but their sin had to be punished. And so it is today. Our sin nature still exists and, unless we repent and get right with God, we too will be exiled from God's Garden of Eden, forever separated from His loving arms.

Man lives today the same way Adam and Eve wanted to live in the garden. They want to be like God, therefore they want to be in control of their own lives and not have God control theirs. Proverbs 14:12 says, *"There is a way that appears to be right to man, but in the end it leads to death." NIV.* Man, in his own wisdom, thinks there is a way to go in life that appears right but isn't. That Amplified Bible talks about a way that seems *"straight"* to man. Why does it appear to be right? It appears to be right because they have a worldview through their own lenses or how they perceive the world to be without checking how God views the world through His lenses — His Holy Word.

We have then come to have our own perspective of life and how we should react to a certain set of circumstances instead of a biblical perspective or how God sees it from His own perspective. If everyone else is going the same way, doing the same thing, then it must seem right. It appears that way so it must be the right way. When we take that perspective we begin to look at our circumstances through our own skewed, dark, cloudy and sin-filled eyes and, upon surveying the situation, we decide what is right and what is wrong. All of it is apart from God's guidance, wisdom, and direction, and the end result, apart from God's view or perspective, only leads to death.

Asaph, who fulfilled the role of David's musical director in the Old Testament, and wrote twelve psalms, recounted in Psalm 73 how man seemed to prosper when viewed through his own eyes. He saw the prosperity of the wicked when he said, *"For I was envious of the boastful, when I 'saw' the prosperity of the wicked." V.3 NKJV.* They didn't serve God, but they were those who only acknowledged God when ridiculing and cursing Him. *"They set their mouths against the heavens,"* and *"And they say, 'How does God know? And is there knowledge in the Most High?'" NKJV.* He saw through his own eyes that the wicked prospered, cursed God, were healthy, and even oppressed others, but they SEEMED to be well according to his own perspective, his own worldview.

Asaph confessed that he had almost slipped, he nearly became like one of them, someone living in the world apart from God's guidance and direction. He served God in his daily walk but seemed to experience nothing but pain and heartache; he wasn't prosperous; he toiled long and hard without any results. He said, *"For all day long I have been plagued, and chastened (disciplined) every morning." V.14 NKJV.*

Asaph tried, in his own strength, through his own worldview, to understand what was happening before him, but it was too overwhelming for him, too painful to consider or even understand. Nothing seemed to make sense. People prosper and are healthy and do well, despite the fact they don't serve God and, in fact, curse him. This would seem to be the case if we are viewing situations in our lives through our own lenses and not through God's lenses.

But when Asaph began to view the situation through God's perspective, then and only then, did he begin to understand their tragic end. He continued, *"When I thought how to understand this, it was too painful for me — Until I went into the sanctuary of God; Then I understood their end." V. 16-17. NKJV.* When he saw the situation through his own eyes and what appeared to be right to him, he simply couldn't understand what he was seeing, but when he had personal contact or relationship with God, when he spent that special time with Him and sought His perspective, he began to view the situation through God's lenses; he began to see the situation before him much more clearly! There was a certain revelation, a certain piece of knowledge missing when this situation was viewed in his own understanding.

Asaph began to see through God's lenses the wicked people's eventual end. They were doomed to destruction, that *"those who are from You shall perish; You will destroy all who are false to You and like [spiritual] harlots depart from You." V. 27. AMP.*

Any viewpoint in the world apart from viewing it through God's eyes may seem right at that time, but its end is certain death. We in the church also fall victim to the world's way. We view the world and how they live their lives through our own lenses and make our own assumptions, determinations, and judgments based on what we see, but it is all folly; it's untrue; it's not biblical because it isn't seen through the eyes of God. Once the world is viewed through God's eyes, everything we view changes its focus; it becomes clearer and easier to understand. We begin to view the world as God does; a world that is entrenched firmly in sin and in need of a Savior. It's a world destined to destruction and that will perish because they live apart from His wisdom, grace, and love, only desiring to see the world as they choose to see it.

Isaiah was a prophet who was commissioned and ordained of God to speak His Word, His truth, to His people who were living in sin, and God anointed him to warn them of their impending disaster. Isaiah's words, much of the time, were words of confrontation and warning, which were unpopular to hear and receive, especially when the Israelites were in exile in Babylon.

God was angry with His people for their sexual immorality, disobedience, and idolatry. Isaiah also spoke of the promise and hope that would be extended to His people if they repented of their sinful ways and returned to God. Oh where are our Isaiah's in the church in America today? Where are the pastors who need to speak the truth of God's Word, who will confront people in sin when necessary, who will warn His people of their impending disaster if they continue in their immoral and idolatrous ways?

Isaiah tried to warn anyone who would listen that their sin would bring forth God's judgment. Despite his message being unpopular and unwelcomed by God's people, he continued to speak the truth as God had ordained him, no matter who was willing to listen. He didn't conform to society's demands to change. He wasn't willing to rewrite the truth just to comfort the people who were hurting or because it was politically correct to do so. He spoke the truth because God demanded that His truth be spoken and he knew this, despite the overwhelming hostilities he faced among his people.

The Israelites were just like those in the church today. They lived life according to the way they felt it should be lived, despite witnessing God's blessings time and time again, hence Isaiah's warning. God's people were on their road to destruction because of their own view of the world, their own view of what they thought to be right and wrong or good and evil.

In Chapter 5 in the book of Isaiah, Isaiah talked about the Israelites being God's disappointing vineyard, and he exhorted them to get themselves right before God. His words were certainly confrontational and depressing, but they didn't have to be that way if the people had just listened to him as a man who heard from God. In verse 20, Isaiah said, *"You are doomed! You call evil good and call good evil. You turn darkness into light and light into darkness. You make what is bitter sweet, and what is sweet you make bitter." GNB*. He also stated in the next verse,

"Woe to those who are wise in their own eyes and prudent and shrewd in their own sight." AMP.

Isaiah was warning them to turn back to God, to remember how He delivered them out of every situation they were in, despite punishment that had to be endured because of their sinful ways. All was not lost; they were still not out of the reach of God's forgiveness and mercy, and neither are we.

Isaiah warned that apart from God we are confused and make wrong choices that seem right, but aren't. God's people couldn't decipher truth from falsehood, what they considered good was evil and evil was good. And that's exactly what we do in the church today. We say it's good for homosexuals and lesbians to marry because they love each other and believe they are born that way, and whatever other excuses we may say in the church, so their lifestyle choices are accepted. We say it's good for those couples who live together outside the covenant of marriage because that's what everyone else does, or they need some time to live together before they decide if marriage will work. We say it's good to give contraceptives to those who are having sex because abstinence is non-existent. We say everyone else is having sex, so why attempt to offer them a healthier, alternate lifestyle? We, the church, in essence, have become a pluralistic society. A pluralistic society is defined as a theory that there are multiple realities, rather than one ultimate reality. A society defined this way means that whatever you feel is right within your own set of moral guidelines must be right and accepted. But that theory simply isn't true, so the church must stand against this. There is only one truth that exists, and that truth is Jesus Christ.

We in the church say it's evil to allow a former prisoner, a homosexual or lesbian, homeless person, alcoholic, drug addict, divorcee, tattooed individual into the church because we say they're different from us. "Who are these sinners?" we cry out as we pound our chests in arrogance. We don't want that individual, that vile sinner to corrupt or intervene in our pure and unadulterated worship service! We, in fact, have corrupted the church when we cast judgments upon those whom God loves too. Apart from God, we know no good but only evil. Apart from God, we adopt a worldview, a view from our own eyes, and bring those views into the church despite His warning that He will judge those *"who are wise in their own eyes."*

Who is good and determines what is good? God is the only one who knows and performs well. He has chosen us as His vessels to perform good in and through us. When God created the earth, He saw through His own lenses what was good. When God had seen the earth without form and void and dark, He commanded that there be light and there was light. *"And God saw that the light was GOOD (suitable, pleasant) and He approved it; and God separated light from the darkness." Gen. 1:4. AMP.*

God determined then what was good. He determined what was good through what He created and saw, through His own power and judgment. God had decided what was good before man ever came into existence. He has determined what is good from eternity past, and what is good is left up to Him to decide. The Scripture also stated that what God saw was not only good, but that He, in His infinite wisdom, approved of His own handiwork.

As God continued to create the Earth, the dry land and the seas, the birds of the air and the creatures of the land and sea, He also created the light and the darkness and the stars in the sky, and the sun and moon and the trees that bore fruit and saw that it was all good. Each day brought with it new promise because all of God's handiwork is good when He alone determines what is good.

He was pleased and approved of His creation. However, there was something still missing, something that required His plan to be fulfilled, and that plan was to create us. We completed His perfect plan. He had chosen us to be keepers of the earth, to rule it wisely. We are the only creation created in His likeness and image. *"So God created man in His own image, in the image and likeness of God he created him; male and female He created them."* Gen. 1:27. AMP.

As God had completed the heavens and the earth on the sixth day, the Scripture in Genesis 1 verse 31 states that God previewed all that He had made and determined that all was not only good, but it was VERY good! All that exists was created by Him and He was well-pleased with His creation, especially the creation of man. He had desired that we be His righteous and moral representation on this earth and that we, created in His image and likeness, would reflect Him on earth. He had given man tremendous responsibility because *"everyone to whom much was given, of him much will be required."* Lk. 12:48. ESV.

God had provided us all that we would ever need and desire. We were loved, protected, and blessed. But when Satan came disguised as a serpent and deceived Adam and Eve, life as they knew it would be forever changed. Sin, our self-indulgent need, entered into our bloodstream. The perfect man was now broken, damaged, as the poison of sin flowed through his veins and bloodstream!

Sin forever altered our thinking, our emotions, and our actions. We were now stained with guilt and the depravity of sin. What God had determined was good by His standard of goodness was usurped by man, but what man now thinks to be good and wise simply isn't good or wise, but evil and folly.

Dwelling within His Garden of Eden, His paradise, was now a corrupt and sinful people. God's creation, with whom He was well-pleased and which was good, was no longer good and He wasn't pleased. He pronounced judgment upon their sin, as they were no longer able to partake anymore of all the beauty He had created within that garden. He cast them out. Wow! What a judgment upon the human race because of our sin, but thanks be to God that He still protected them, He still loved them, and He didn't destroy them, which He certainly could have done!

God is pronouncing judgment upon His church as He did in the garden, due to our sin too. He has to. We aren't pleased with all He has extended and given to us. We want to continue to eat of the forbidden fruit and do things our way and through our own eyes and expect God to turn a blind eye to it all. He can't and He won't! He didn't turn a blind eye to Adam and Eve's sin, and He won't turn a blind eye to our sins either. He pronounced judgment upon them and He will pronounce judgment upon us. We can't escape it. We can't run and hide from it. We have to face the sins we commit in our lives or face the consequences.

Chapter 14

God's Desire for Visitation in His Church

We have all that we could ever need or desire in God, as Adam and Eve did. They had a perfect, pure, and unadulterated relationship with God. It was harmonious and peaceful. They enjoyed and desired His presence as He desired theirs. He had made His visitation to them and with them, and He dwelled with them and them with Him, but one act of disobedience changed it all. They became a sinful and imperfect race. They were no longer pure but fully stained with the wretchedness of sin. They no longer had an unadulterated relationship with God, but they became spiritual adulteresses. They cheated on God, preferring to cavort with the enemy and fulfill their own fleshly, carnal desires through him instead. What a tragic decision they made! It was a decision that forever changed the human race. One fatal act of selfishness alienated man forever from having that pure, perfect, and unadulterated relationship with God Himself! What a tragic mistake indeed!

They lost that personal visitation they had with God in favor of Satan's visitation. Jesus stated the same to His people as He made His triumphal entry into Jerusalem. What was to be a joyous celebration of our King's entrance into Jerusalem culminated in a tremendous weeping over that very city!

As Jesus road on a donkey into Jerusalem, He was overwhelmed with emotion. He wept over the city because the love He showed to His people would be rejected. Luke 19 and verses 41-44 in The Amplified Bible version really capture beautifully the emotions of our Savior.

"And as He approached, He saw the city, and He wept [audibly] over it, exclaiming, "Would that you had known personally, even at least in this your day, the things that make for peace (for freedom from all the distresses that are experienced as the result of sin and upon which your peace — your security, safety, prosperity, and happiness — depends)! But now they are hidden from your eyes. For a time is coming upon you when your enemies will throw up a bank [with pointed stakes] about you and surround you and shut you in on every side."

"And they will dash you to the ground, you [Jerusalem] and your children within you; and they will not leave in you one stone upon another, [all] because you did not come progressively to recognize and know and understand [from observation and experience] the time of your visitation [that is, when God was visiting you, the time in which God showed Himself gracious toward you and offered you salvation through Christ]."

Imagine Jesus weeping over the city of Jerusalem as He is weeping over the church in America today! Jesus didn't just shed a few crocodile tears! He was overcome with sorrow and emotion. He wept audibly; His whole body was wracked with emotion and tears. Weeping is defined as a fit or spell of shedding tears. Our Lord was weeping and could be heard weeping by those gathered around him as He rode on His donkey into the city. He saw the sins of His very people, and He had given them the opportunity to repent. He had visited them, dwelt among them, ministered God's love to them, healed every kind of disease and sickness, yet they still rejected their Son, their Savior, to indulge their own sins, their self-indulgent needs!

Jesus is weeping; He is overcome with emotions because of the sin-filled church in America that He witnesses today. The church, His body, which is supposed to be a separate people beholden to Him, a people commanded to spread the Gospel in all the earth and to make disciples to follow Him, is failing miserably and, as a result, the church as we know it is close to extinction, close to death, lying on its bed of iniquity and on life support due to the lack of moral conviction to do what's right according to what His Word commands. The church has knelt in agreement to the world's demands just like His people were doing in Jerusalem, and it affected Christ to the point of weeping!

Jesus was overlooking the vast expanse of the city as He looks over the vast expanse of America. I could imagine our Lord witnessing the people of the city going about their business without any concern for their eternal destination. He witnessed sin among His people because He said that He desired that they had known Him personally, that God in the flesh was among them, but they were too blinded by their sins to even realize it.

The Amplified Bible stated that Jesus desired that they would know Him and experience His peace, the peace or freedom that would result from being forgiven for their sin-filled lives. It's the sin of man that causes all kinds of heartache and distresses, and it's those very sins that are destroying the church, because the church is His people who should be coming together to be His hands and feet in this sin-infested world.

To have that true peace, security, safety, prosperity, and happiness He desired for Jerusalem and in turn desires for us, we need to be saved, washed anew in His blood. However, Christ said that His people are blinded to the truth found in Him, that His truth had become hidden from them because of their sin. See, sin can't see the light but only darkness. When we're involved in sin, we're blinded from the truth; it's hidden from us despite Jesus standing right there in front of us, willing to remove our sin-filled garments. How we view situations is only through darkness; it's viewed only through the lenses of sin.

When we view things through the lenses of sin, we miss Jesus! We can't and won't see Him! *"The lamp of the body is the eye. If therefore your eye is good, your whole body will be full of light." Matt.*

6:22 NKJV. We filter the world through our eyes, and if our eyes are the eyes of Jesus, then our eyes are good and we'll be full of the light found in Him! Jesus doesn't say just to view things through our eyes, but He first asks IF those eyes are GOOD eyes, meaning that some eyes are evil and only have darkness within them.

John 3:18-21 is an excellent example Jesus gives about light and darkness. *"He who believes in Him is not condemned; but he who does not believe is condemned already, because he has not believed in the name of the only begotten Son of God." NKJV.* The Amplified Bible says that those who believe are those who cling to, trust in, and rely on Him and Him alone. That's why Jesus wept. He saw and sees people today who don't cling to, trust in, or rely on Him for their salvation, for Him to deliver from or to take them through their trials in this life.

He talks about those who are not condemned and are not judged. The Amplified Bible states that whoever believes or trusts in Christ never comes up for judgment, that there will be no rejection of God for that person. He will incur no condemnation or damnation.

If we don't believe in the name of Christ, we're condemned. Jesus goes on to explain in the Scripture what this condemnation is all about. *"And this is the condemnation, that the light has come into the world, and men [people] have loved darkness rather than the light, because their deeds were evil."* As was stated earlier, any attempt at any work outside of God's guidance, wisdom, and direction, is only evil.

"For everyone practicing evil hates the light and does not come to the light, lest his deeds should be exposed. But he who does the truth comes to the light, that his deeds may be clearly seen, that they have been done in God." Jesus is the light who has come into the world. He has visited His people in Jerusalem and He has visited His people here in America.

Jesus grieved because His time of visitation was rejected. He knew His city would be destroyed and it was. They were eventually annihilated and in ruins because they rejected His visitation. They didn't recognize or know and understand who was among them, despite their plethora of miraculous experiences with the King. God had indeed been gracious to His people because He gave His one and only Son to suffer and die a terrible death for the sins of the people.

Jesus had given them an opportunity to repent and to recognize that He was and is the light who offered salvation, but they didn't receive Him. He had offered them a new way of life, a life far better than their sin-scarred life, a life that would have given them eternal life in and through Him, but they wanted none of it.

These were the same people who tried to stone Jesus for saying He and God were one and that He had the authority and power to not only lay down His life for them, but to be able to take it back, or rise up, again. A dispute arose among them as to whether Jesus was indeed God in the flesh or some crazy loon who was a blasphemous liar. John 10 recounts this incident with His own people when he recounts how they circled Jesus and demanded that He tell them whether He was really the Christ, the Messiah they had been waiting for. He spoke in parables, which only frustrated them, and even more so when He claimed His deity. They attempted to stone Him to death.

When He again stated in verse 38 that He and the Father were one, they attempted to arrest Him, but He escaped. Finally let's look at Luke 4. After Jesus had been baptized by John the Baptist in the River Jordan, He was led by the Holy Spirit into the wilderness for forty days and forty nights, as God prepared His Son for what He was going to face from His own chosen people and within His ministry.

Jesus experienced a time of preparation in the desert that left Him physically weary and tempted by the devil. He not only survived this experience, but He thrived in the circumstances of life, because the

Scriptures teach us He left the wilderness empowered in the Holy Spirit.

Jesus had begun teaching in their synagogues and was praised, recognized, and honored among the people. His ministry was growing rapidly and His fame spread throughout the region. He was probably invited to speak to His people at their synagogue in Nazareth, the place where He grew up, a place where He was known very well.

Jesus had read a portion of Scripture from Isaiah before He sat down. Luke recounts that the congregation were gazing attentively at Him. "What will He say to us, His people?" they probably wondered. "We must be special because He has visited us in our synagogue. He grew up here among us. We know His mom and dad. All of these great miracles that He has performed in the other towns and regions must be nothing compared to what He will show us in His time and visitation with us." They waited with baited anticipation for what Jesus was going to do among them. It's also probably safe to say that there were many people with diseases and illnesses who were in the congregation that day.

Jesus said to them, *"Today this Scripture has been fulfilled while you are present and hearing." Lk. 4:21 (AMP)*. Jesus was referring to Isaiah 61:1-2, which Jesus stated had referred to Him as the One Isaiah was speaking about, the Messiah who was anointed to preach the Good news or Gospel to the poor, to release those who were in captivity, to give sight to those who were blind, to deliver those who were oppressed, and to proclaim the accepted and acceptable year of the Lord. It would be the day when salvation and God's grace would come upon His people bountifully!

The people were in amazement and *"marveled at the words of grace that came forth from His mouth." V.22. (AMP)* They even asked if this is truly Joseph's son, the son of a middle-class carpenter? Is this really the boy we saw running around in the neighborhood and watched grow up before our eyes, and who worked with His dad and had no formal education?

Could He really be the Messiah, the One we've been waiting for? They were stunned and filled with amazement. Wow! This Jesus has come to us, His people in His community! What will He do for us?

But Jesus' visitation was about to be cut short. In a few short moments, the Jesus they marveled at with amazement, the Jesus they said was so good that they spoke so highly of Him, the Jesus who spoke words of grace from His mouth, would soon be ridiculed, cursed at, hated, and nearly thrown off a cliff! His time of visitation had ended. Why? What happened so quickly that His own people from His own community would want to kill Him? Why were they filled with all of these negative emotions?

SIN!

They refused to hear or accept what He had to say. He knew the hearts of the people: the pride, arrogance, and we-are-better-than-them attitude. What did He say that angered them so much that they wanted to kill Him? Jesus told them about two prophets, Elijah and Elisha, who ministered to two Gentiles, one a widow, and the other Naaman the Syrian. He performed miracles in their lives but not in the lives of His chosen people, the Israelites, because of their sin, their hardness of heart. The two people He had healed had put their faith and trust in God for their healing and deliverance.

After Jesus had spoken those two references, indicating He would do no healing among His people because of their spiritual pride, they became incensed. *"When they heard these things, all the people in the synagogue were filled with rage." V.28 (AMP)*. What were they expecting? Were they expecting Jesus to make a mockery of His miracles and healings just for their witness? Was this some kind of show just for their benefit so they could say that the miracles and healings in their church were better than some other church's healings? Or were they claiming to be a special people because Jesus grew up in their community, and expecting to claim Him as their own, and when they found out He didn't belong to any specific group, culture or region, they became enraged?

Whatever the reason, they were angry and hateful. His visitation was no longer welcome. They chose darkness instead of light. *"And rising up, they pushed and drove him out of the town, and [laying hold of Him] they led him to the [projecting] upper part of the hill on which their town was built, that they might hurl Him headlong down [over the cliff]. But passing through their midst, He went on His way." V. 29-30. (AMP)*. Wow! The same people who invited Jesus into their church, who marveled at His words and grace and were speaking well of Him, suddenly weren't interested in listening to His Words and acknowledging their sins and taking the action necessary to change their lives for the better; to see the error of their ways, to repent, and be forgiven by Jesus Himself. They wouldn't listen.

The same Jesus they rejected in the synagogue, it could be argued, is the same Jesus the church rejects today. Why? Because we each have our own ideas of who Jesus should be to us. We look at Him through our own worldly, sinful lenses and assume He is this all-loving, all-merciful God who doesn't confront sin but forgives all no matter what we do. We see Jesus as someone who must respond to all of our requests, whether it's a request lined up with His will or a request to fill our own insatiable desire to fulfill our own self-indulgent needs, and we expect Him to respond immediately to all of them.

We have created a microwave Jesus in this fast-paced, no patience, hectic existence we call life, and we want what we want now in this society in which we now live. If someone is of no benefit to us, we just cast them aside as yesterday's garbage, and the church just stands idly by, refusing to address this grievous issue with their people because they're in bondage to them, which in effect binds us to the enemy.

The Jews had their own vision of who Jesus should be to them instead of what Jesus wants us to be to and for Him! He was this guy who was from their neighborhood who had been performing amazing miracles, so they had envisioned Him to be someone who would do even more for them, and that He belonged to them. Since they had their own image of who He should be through their own sinful lenses, they couldn't bear to accept the fact that Jesus was trying to change them!

We cry that we don't need to change, but that Jesus needs to change and conform to our expectations and desires for Him. However, the Scripture is clear that *"Jesus is the same yesterday and today, and forever." Heb. 13:8. NIV.* We are the ones who need to change and not Him. He has come to change us from the inside out, as He has come *"to seek and save the lost." Lk.19:10. NIV.*

Chapter 15

Cure for Sin

So the question cries out: What are we to do? Is all hope lost? Will we continue to move away from God in the church as the sin continues to destroy it? The sin, our self-indulgent needs, have laid the church in America on its death bed, clinging to life support. There are those who will look across the landscape of America as Jesus did over Jerusalem and cry that it's over, there's no hope left. The church is going to die! It's lying on its sickbed with barely a heartbeat as the life of the church continues to ebb out of its pores. The poison of sin, the cancer that it is, continues to inject itself within the church's veins without any sign of it changing course, and the poison is killing it!

Others may look and say, "NO, it's not over." Yes, I see with my natural eyes that things are indeed not good, in fact, by all accounts, the prognosis is terrible. We weep as Jesus wept over the city of Jerusalem and its people and wonder what happened. We wonder how things got to the place that they are here in America, and we begin to ask what we could do to change course. How could we save the church from death? Could we really save it? Should we listen to the doctor, Satan, and accept the medications he has prescribed, which are filled with his deceptions and lies, and like Adam and Eve did give in to the devil's temptation to quit? Should we question God's judgment and Word and listen to Satan's whispers that the church won't indeed die and that all is great?

The answer is that all hope is not yet lost! There is still a chance for the church to rise up from its bed of iniquity. Yes, time is short, but there is still time to

Cure for Sin

heal the sin and poison that has left it nearly lifeless! We ask what could be done. Is there some magic cure out there that would heal the church at this stage of the process of the disease? There is a cure, but it's not a magical cure. It's a cure rained down from heaven and instilled in the hearts of people, the church. It's the only antidote available that, if injected into the veins of the church, will strengthen it once again, that will cause it to rise up stronger than it's ever been and heal it from all the disease of sin that has wasted its body away.

If there's a cure and antidote that will heal the church, then what is it? What exists that could be injected into its nearly lifeless body that will make it well again? Has it rained down from heaven and is it available right now? If so, then what is it? The answer is quite simple. This antidote has been available from eternity past, but we haven't exercised it fully within the church. Why? Because if it's a truly penetrable antidote and it's applied to the church in America, then it will become a strong church that sin will never topple. In fact, sin and the embodiment of sin, Satan, would have to flee from it. This cure can't co-exist with sin because sin would no longer be allowed to enter the church body to wrack it with poison any longer.

This antidote is so strong there is nothing that sin could do to penetrate the church. It will be impervious to the pain of sin. If this antidote is pumping through the very veins of the church, it will grow and spread throughout the church in such force and strength that it will become a force that is undefeatable.

The antidote that will combat and defeat sin, the antidote that will reverse the terrible, destructive sickness enveloping the church in America today and heal it totally and completely is simply: LOVE!! Yes! It is not the earthly love that we understand or speak of today, but it's the love that *"has been poured out in our hearts through the Holy Spirit Who has been given to us." Rom. 5:5. AMP.* The love named here is God's love, the perfect, sinless, unadulterated love that has been poured into our hearts, the church body in America, by God Himself!

God's love is the perfect cure for what ails the church today! It's the love that was sent down to earth from the perfection of heaven in the form of a man to suffer and die a terrible death, and His name is Jesus Christ! *"For God so greatly loved and dearly prized the world that He [even] gave up His only begotten (unique) Son, so that whoever believes in (trusts in, clings to, relies on) Him shall not perish (come to destruction, be lost) but have eternal (everlasting life)." Jn. 3:16 AMP.*

It's the love that God has for all of us, that He would send His one and only Son to suffer and die for our sins placed upon His body on the cross at Calvary! What a love indeed! A Father who gave up His Son for us because of His tremendous love for us. A Father who loves us so much that Jesus would cry out in anguish when His own Father had forsaken Him as He bore the sins of us all upon the cross at

Calvary! Oh how heart wrenching that must have been for the Father.

Let's take some time to explore this great gift of love, the gift that has been rejected by millions of people within the church body today. It's a gift that is still extended to us and available to us, if we would accept that gift of love found in the personhood of Jesus Christ. However, something else needs to take place first in the very heart of man before they can receive this love extended to us. The church in America first needs a heart transplant!

Chapter 16

A Transplanted Heart

The current state of the heart in the church is filled with sin, so before love is allowed to take root in the lifeblood of the church, it needs a heart transplant. Love injected into the veins of the church and mixed with sin won't cure what ails the church. Like a natural heart pumps blood into our bloodstream, we can't prosper the way God intends us to prosper when there's a disease infiltrating our body. A new and clean heart has to be inserted into the body of the church. Why? Because the heart has been so weakened and destroyed by centuries of sin, the new heart must work with the antidote of love, to pump it into the lifeblood of the church to produce a long, prosperous, and successful life. God spoke to the prophet Ezekiel about His people, the church, regarding their need for a new heart that would revive His people from their deathbed of sin when He said, "I will give you a new heart and put a new spirit within you; I will take the heart of stone out of your flesh and give you a heart of flesh. I will put My Spirit within you and cause you to walk in My statutes, and you will keep my judgments and do them." Ezek. 36:26-27. NKJV. God desires to remove that heart of stone which has become hardened due to sin and replace it with a heart of flesh, a heart of love that will be ready for Him to place His Holy Spirit within it that will purpose us to live this life the way He desires us to live it within the church and our personal lives.

David spoke of needing a new heart and he requested that God would create a new heart within him, a heart devoted to the will of God and not himself. He recognized he was a sinner and needed a change of heart. That's what we, as a body of believers, need as well before any sustaining and eternal life can flow through the body of Jesus Christ — His church!

Why did David write Psalm 51? What was his reason for doing so? David came to the point, when confronted with his sin that he repented and asked God for a new, clean heart! First, David had to recognize the sin in his life and be willing to deal with it quickly and harshly.

David was a king who was mightily blessed by God. He was hand-chosen by God to lead His people. He had much territory and possessions and was even described as a man after God's own heart, and he was a mostly righteous king, until sin seeped into his life when his eyes beheld a married woman named Bathsheba. He saw her bathing when he was walking on the roof of his palace and *"saw that she was beautiful to behold."* He was looking at her lustfully, through his own natural, sinful eyes and not the eyes of God, and desired to be with her in a sexual manner.

Bathsheba's husband, Uriah, was away at battle for King David, so David took advantage of the opportunity and committed adultery by sleeping with Bathsheba. She became pregnant with his child, but that wasn't the end of his sin. He tried to cover it up by sending Uriah home from battle and encouraging him to sleep with his wife, so he could make it look like it had been Uriah who had impregnated his wife. Uriah didn't accept the king's offer. He wanted to be back with his men on the battlefield. So King David conjured up an evil, maniacal plan to cover his sin. He ordered that Uriah be positioned in the front lines on the battlefield, assuring his death! And that's exactly what happened! Uriah was killed in battle.

Trying to cover up one sin with another sin and another one after that doesn't hide our sin. It only entrenches us deeper into our sins and further away from God's mercy and truth. We need the sin exposed for the heart transplant to occur. The sin must be gotten rid of. It must be exposed in Christ's light. *"And have no fellowship with the unfruitful works of darkness, but rather expose them. For it is shameful even to speak of those things which are done by them in secret. But all things that exposed are made manifest by the light, for whatever makes manifest is light." Eph. 5:11-13 NKJV.*

David's sin was made manifest, meaning it was revealed, brought forth, and proven through the prophet Nathan. Once David realized his sins and the many lives that were destroyed by his sins and the fact that he had sinned against God, he became grieved. He was broken, crushed, struck down. He realized what he had done and was repentant.

What does it mean to be repentant? For our sin to be properly dealt with, and a heart transplant to take place, we have to first believe that a sin occurred and agree that it has to be dealt with and brought to the light and exposed before God. We have to be so convicted, broken, and grieved for sinning against God and others that we cry out to God as David did, and plead for His forgiveness and mercy. That's what repentance is! It's to admit one's sins and to turn

from those sins and turn **to** God, who will forgive us. It's being so broken because of our sins and the havoc they've caused that we want a change of life; we desire a new, fresh start. God will forgive you.

However, God will more than just forgive us! 1 John 1:9 says in the Amplified Bible that, *"If we [freely] admit that we have sinned and confess our sins, He is faithful and just (true to His own nature and promises) and will forgive our sins [dismiss our lawlessness] and [continuously] cleanse us from all unrighteousness [everything not in conformity to His will in purpose, thought, and action]."*

When we recognize our sins, confess them by repenting of them, then God will not only forgive us, but He will cleanse us from all unrighteousness, that is, all the sins we commit; sins that are, in fact, against God's nature and promises. Everything in purpose, thought, or action that doesn't conform to His will. He will cleanse us from all of it and create within us a new, clean heart!

Returning to Psalm 51, King David admitted that his sins had permeated his body; they had coursed through every vein in his body. He said, *"Behold, I was brought forth in iniquity, and in sin my mother conceived me. Behold, You desire truth in the inward parts, and in the hidden part You will make me to know wisdom." Ps. 51:5-6. NKJV.* What were those sins doing to him? They were killing him from the inside out! He got to the point that he had grieved so tremendously and was broken as a man; all he could do was to cry out to God to forgive him. He wasn't any longer looking at his finances, his beauty, his social status, or his possessions. All he could focus on was the exposed sin before him, and before he could move forward it needed to be confronted.

David cried out in verse 10, *"Create in me a clean heart, O God, and renew a right, persevering, and steadfast spirit within me." AMP.* David repented and asked God to be the one to create within him a new and clean heart. The word "create" used in this verse is the same word used in Genesis 1:1 when God *"created the heavens and the earth." AMP.*

Create is to make or bring into existence something new! God wants to create something new within the church in America today, to raise it from its deathbed existence. And that is to give us a fresh, new and clean heart so He can inject the life of love back into the church. However, we need to recognize our sin, expose it to Christ's light, and deal with it quickly and harshly, despite the pain it may initially bring, by repenting of it and asking God, as David did, to create a new heart within us!

No one said that it would be easy, but without first some serious pain and pressure, a heart transplant can't take place. Sin doesn't want to flee; it doesn't want to leave its comfortable bed of existence within the church today, so it may fight by causing divisions and separations within the church body. But the transplant is required if the church wants to continue its existence within the sinful world around it.

Jeremiah 17 describes the heart in not so flattering terms. The Amplified version cuts to the heart, no pun intended, of what God's Word says about a heart separated from God by sin. *"The heart is deceitful above all things, and it is exceedingly perverse and corrupt and severely, **mortally sick**! Who can know it [perceive, understand, be acquainted with his own heart and mind]?" Jer. 17:9. AMP.* The heart is deceitful above all things, not some things, but all things. There is nothing in this world or universe more deceitful and corruptible than the heart of man! That's why it needs a heart transplant!

The Word speaks of it being not just perverse and corrupt, but being **abundantly** and **exceedingly** perverse, corrupt and severely mortally sick. Anything mortally wounded or sick dies! And the heart of the church, unless transplanted with a new heart, can't and won't survive! It will die!

Further, Jesus described in vivid detail the heart of man when He stated in Matthew 13:15, *"For this nation's heart has grown gross (fat and dull), and* *their ears heavy and difficult of hearing, and their eyes they have tightly closed, lest they see and perceive with their eyes, and hear and comprehend with the sense of their ears, and grasp and understand with their heart, and **turn** and I should heal them." AMP.* Jesus was describing what Isaiah had mentioned about the state of God's people and His impending judgment upon them due to their sin.

Who can truly understand the heart of man except God Himself? God knows that our heart is desperately wicked and evil and something needs to be done about it. Jesus described in Mark 7:20 what proceeds from the heart of man when He said, *"What comes out of a person is what defiles them. For it is from within, out of a person's HEART, that evil thoughts come — sexual immorality, theft, murder, adultery, greed, malice, deceit, lewdness, envy, slander, arrogance and folly. All these evils come from inside and defile a person." NIV.*

Every form of evil known to man emanates from our hearts. It all begins in our heart and flows from within the heart and courses through our entire being and eventually flows out of us. Having a heart change or heart transplant is crucial to receiving God's love. Having a heart given over to God for Him to replace will begin a new relationship with Him based on love, which in turn will radically change the church for His glory.

Let's take a look at how God dealt with His people in the desert through their leader, Moses. God desired to bless them as He wants to bless us, but they had to fear Him and to walk in obedience to Him and to love and serve Him with their entire being. However, God knew it was impossible for the Israelites to honor His commands without a heart transplant.

He described how He created and owns the heavens, even the highest heavens, and the earth and everything in it, but He chose to love and to bless and to shower His <u>affection</u> upon His chosen people more than anyone else because of His <u>love</u> for and His promises to their ancestors. However,

He said the following was required for them to fulfill His commands: *"Circumcise your hearts, therefore, and do not be a stiff-necked people any longer." Deut.10:16. AMP.*

God stated later in Chapter 30 that it wasn't too late for His people to repent and receive a new heart, and then they would be accepted by Him. So there's still hope for the church in America today! He promised many blessings to those who returned to Him when He began in verse 1, *"And when these things come upon you…and shall return to the Lord your God and obey His voice according to all that I command you today, you and your children, with all your [mind and] heart and with all your being, then the Lord your God will restore your fortunes and have compassion upon you and will gather you again from all the nations where He has scattered you."* Verse 6, *"And the Lord your God will circumcise your hearts and the hearts of your descendants, to love the Lord your God with all your [mind and] heart and with all your being, that you may live." AMP.*

A Transplanted Heart

God says that we must repent, circumcise our hearts (experience a heart transplant), and THEN we will live. Why? Because then we will be able to receive His love that He has stored up for us, which will enable us to love Him with our entire being and in turn love others with the loves He bestows on us!

That's it! The antidote of love will be injected into the church body when we have a heart transplant. We must allow the surgeon Jesus to perform the surgery. Suppose you visit the doctor because you're not feeling well. You feel weak and short of breath and decide to see what's wrong. Your doctor runs a series of tests and discovers you have several blocked arteries. He then sends you to a cardiologist for further examination. The cardiologist then discovers that not only do you have blocked arteries, but you are diagnosed with coronary artery disease, which requires a heart transplant.

What would you do? You may decide to seek a second opinion before deciding your next course of action. If a heart transplant is required for you to live, not just any life, but a quality life, you would decide to receive a new heart. However, you would want to make sure the heart surgeon is highly regarded, perhaps that he's even performed many surgeries in his career, which resulted in a very high success rate. You wouldn't go to just any heart surgeon, but the best you could possibly get. Well, Jesus is the best heart surgeon we would ever need. He comes highly qualified, has a 100 percent success rate, and even promises a life lived to the fullest!

Jesus is our perfect surgeon. We must decide if we need a new heart and, if so, repent and ask Him to create a new heart within us, and then entrust ourselves to Him to perform that perfect surgery: a surgery without failure, a surgery that has succeeded every single time. He will place that new heart within the church body so it can receive the injection of love.

Although a person receiving a new heart has to be hospitalized for some time to be sure the body doesn't reject the new heart, we never have to worry about our body rejecting our new heart, because it would be a heart that's pure and strong and ready to receive His love. It will be implanted within us with love from the perfect surgeon.

Since a new heart implanted by Jesus NEVER gets rejected, it comes to life immediately. Now that the heart is ready to receive the injection of love, what will that love do to the body and for the body? What is this antidote of love? What would it cause the heart of man to do once it's injected with Christ's love?

Chapter 17

Biblical Love

*L*et's take a serious look at what biblical love is all about. Let's see when biblical love, injected into the veins of the church in America, will do to the church body. God's love described in Scripture isn't the kind of love described in society today. The biblical love described is far higher and more powerful than the love we know or think we may know.

The kind of love that God has for each one of us is described in the Greek as agape. Agape love is the highest form of love; it's a love extended without conditions required of the receiving party. We are loved simply because we are who we are and we're loved despite our sins. This is the kind of love extended to us through Jesus Christ's sacrificial death upon the cross.

Imagine that. Jesus, despite our sin-filled lives, gave up His own life so that we may experience life; not just a life here on earth, but a life for eternity with Him. If that isn't a pure, selfless, unadulterated, no conditions attached love, then what is? There is no replacement for the love of Christ as He hung upon that cross. There is absolutely nothing you could do to earn or warrant His love for you. It's simply there for the taking, for us to receive that love given to us to extend to others, too.

Romans 5:8 says, *"But God demonstrates His own love for us in this: While we were still sinners Christ died for us." NIV.* Love has to be demonstrated, it has to be shown or given or extended. Love is an action word that, when flowing through the life of the church, will begin to infect that body in a pure, sinless, and heartfelt way.

God has given that example of love in the personhood of His Son, Jesus Christ. His love is demonstrated to us through His Son. What an amazing love indeed! *"For God so greatly loved and dearly prized the world that He [even] gave up His only begotten [unique] Son, so that whoever believes in (trusts in, clings to, relies on) Him shall not perish (come to destruction, be lost) but have eternal (everlasting) life." Jn.3:16 AMP.*

God freely gave His own Son to die for us! He didn't have to, but He did, simply because of His tremendous and unwavering love for us. He so desires a relationship with us that He had to sacrifice His Son instead of sacrificing us. We don't deserve the love of God. Because of our sin, we deserve death. We deserve to be placed upon that cross of shame; we deserve to be humiliated and put to death for our transgressions, but God, in His love, chose His own Son instead! We will never understand the immense magnitude of Christ's act, but we don't have to understand it. We only have to accept it as a loving and merciful God who loves us so intimately and personally that He wants a relationship of love with us through His Son, Jesus Christ.

That's the agape love that God displayed to us. It's that love already poured out that needs to be demonstrated in our lives and in the life of the church. We don't need to try to reinvent love or try to determine for ourselves what love is, because love that has a set of conditions attached for us to receive that person's love isn't love at all. It's deception and selfishness disguised as love. True love is sacrificial, it's never ending; it's not based on our feelings and emotions on any given day. True godly love hung upon the cross at Calvary, so we need to look no further than the cross to see that love personified in Jesus!

1 Corinthians 13 is a popular and beautiful description of the love God requires of each of us. It's the agape love that exists in those who love God. Love is the only element of our lives, when exercised fully and righteously and purely, that will never die.

It will always be evident because God is love and His love is eternal.

The Amplified version of 1 Corinthians 13 and verse 13 describes love as *"true affection for God and man, growing out of God's love for and in us."* Although faith and hope need to abide in the heart of every believer and are crucial elements of our faith walk, love is the greatest of all three. The Word states this because faith and hope can't exist without love. How could we say we have a wholehearted trust and faith in God but don't express His love? Is faith evident then? How could we say we abide in hope in Jesus Christ and look forward with great hope and expectation to our eternal life in Him, but don't express His love to His children? Is hope evident? Love has to flow within us and then through us for us to experience biblical faith and hope. Faith and hope will flow in abundance where love is evident in Christ's people.

We have God's love in our lives because He has extended His love first to us. 1 John 1:19 says that

"We love Him, because He first loved us." AMP. Without God first extending His love to us through the sacrificial death of His Son, Jesus Christ, it would be impossible for us to love God. Without His love flowing through us and into the lives of His people, we're incapable as sinful humans to truly express godly love. But praise to Him that out of that abundant love extended to us, we can also receive and share it with others. This is truly an amazing, undeserved, selfless, sacrificial, and perfect love!

Chapter 18

The Attributes of God's Love

There are several ways to describe love, but let us particularly look at five attributes of God's love, if you will. God's LOVE is Limitless; it's Overarching; it's Victorious; and finally it is Eternal! The Bible states that God is love. What does that mean, that He is love? It means that love is a central or basic attribute of His Personhood, His character. That doesn't mean that because He is love that it conflicts with His other attributes. His love is the central part or aspect of who He is, and His righteousness, holiness, and judgment, wrath etc., all flow from His character, His love. Every act of God, whether we like it, approve of it, or accept it is always loving, yes even His wrath is extended in love. He is perfect; therefore, His love is perfect, always. Therefore God is love.

Let's take a deeper look into 1 John, the book that delves deeply into God's love for us. It teaches His desire is for us to use that love in the church to revive it from its bed of sin and become the church God has always desired it to be — a church filled with people who love God so deeply and passionately that they extend that pure, selfless love in action within their church body and then in their community, thereby radically changing the community in which they live for Jesus. It is entirely possible because *"with God all things are possible." Matt.19:26. NIV.*

If the love we receive from God through the sacrificial death of His Son, Jesus Christ is poured out into the lives of those around us, the church in America will once again be the proverbial city on the hill with Christ's light shining through in this great land. It will once again be an unstoppable force against the enemy in our neighborhoods and cities across this great land. But the love must be acted upon and our own needs and desires put aside for the needs and desires of God's children. Now that's a godly love that cannot be conquered and will not be stopped; in fact, it will only grow and spread with such ferocity that the devil will flee for his very life.

The book of 1 John explains the kind of love that we need to have to be effective witnesses for Christ. John describes having love for the world and attempting to love God at the same time as an impossible feat because it IS an impossible feat. Verse 15 says this: *"Do not love or cherish the world or the things that are in the world. If anyone loves the world, love for the Father is not in Him."* AMP We cannot love both the world and the Father. It's one or the other, and the choice is ours. Why? Because the world is sinful; it offers us nothing except a sin-filled, wretched, and despicable life that will only lead us to hell for eternity. The love of the world isn't the true, agape love on display in our lives. It's the "what's in it for me?" love, or the "I'll do whatever it takes to get to the top no matter who I need to step on before I get there," miserable life. The world's love is a self-centered, sinful love. So is love of the world love at all? No! It's a deceit and trick by the enemy to lure us into the false notion that our entire actions stem from love, when instead an action or desire that's self-centered is not love. The world's love masquerades itself as love, but it's anything but love. It's SIN! It's a desire to fulfill our own self-indulgent needs, so we either choose the world (darkness) or choose God, who is love (light).

"For all that is in the world — the lust of the flesh [craving for sensual gratification] and the lust of the eyes [greedy longings of the mind] and the pride of life [assurance in one's own resources or in the stability of earthly things] — these do not come from the Father but are from the world [itself]." 1 Jn. 2:15. AMP The world's description of love according to John is fleshly or carnal, it's greedy, and it's prideful. All of these things emanate or are born from the world, and who is the god of this world? Satan!

"Satan, who is the god of this world, has blinded the minds of those who don't believe. They are unable to see the glorious light of the Good News. They don't understand this message about the glory of Christ, who is the exact likeness of God." 2Cor.4:4. NLT

Satan has blinded the minds (hearts) of those within the church. They are unable to see the light, God's love displayed in the death and resurrection of His Son, because they walk in darkness; they are filled to overflowing with the sins of fleshly desires, earthly greed, and pride and are unable to receive and take hold of God's love extended to them.

As stated earlier, the church has allowed the world to creep into it. They have failed to take a stand for Jesus by showing His love to the multitudes, because the world and all of its desires want to destroy the church, and we are letting it happen. How could we then expect the minds and hearts of the people to be ready and willing to receive God's love when they already believe they have it and are expressing it, because the church is saying that worldly love is fine within the church? The congregants are confused as to what godly love is all about. They are getting mixed messages from the pulpit instead of the truth about God's love. They can't tell the difference between worldly love and God's love because they don't see a difference. They've melded them into one form of love and it's destroying the church.

Love isn't the acceptance of someone's lifestyle that is contrary to the Bible. Be it adultery, homosexuality, gay marriage, the practice of sex without being married; to say it's okay because we love them isn't a display of love, but a display of lies. Love IS telling them that it is sin to engage in homosexual acts; it is love to say that abortion is wrong; it is a display of love to tell the leader of your men's ministry that his affair with the secretary is sin. That IS love in action, but the church has allowed God's love to be melded together with the love of the world and it cannot happen. His Word is clear on that.

If we keep within our hearts the message of the cross, which is the message of God's love, we will receive eternal life and be catalysts for change within the church; a change from the world's love, which isn't love at all, to God's love. *"As for you, keep in your hearts what you have heard from the beginning. If what you heard from the first dwells and remains in you, then you will dwell in the Son and the Father [always]. And this is what He Himself has promised us — the life, the eternal [life]." 1 Jn. 2:24-25. AMP*

If we are in a position to receive God's love, we come to understand that His love is limitless. God's love has no end; His love is not conditional. His love is unrestricted. We limit ourselves because we are human, but God is not. He is not bound by time and has no limits. He's from eternity past and eternity future. His love continues without end. His love for us will never cease. Even if there are those who die without Him and face judgment by Him, which will be for an eternity separated from Him, His judgment is still rooted in love. It will always be that way because that is His essence, His being, His character. He is love and that love is limitless!

"Now to Him who is able to do immeasurably more than all we ask or imagine, according to His power that is at work within us." Eph.3:20. NIV. We can't measure God's love in us. It's too vast or too big to ever place a limit on it, and that is an awesome God we serve. God is able and we need to be ready, willing, and able to receive that love, too. The Scripture in Ephesians says that He will do immeasurably more than we could ever ask or imagine in our finite minds, but He does it according to His power that is within us. That love that is limitless from God is within us. It's not our love that's limitless, but it's His love within us that is limitless, and that love is powerful!

When we read through the Scriptures, we notice how time and again God's love is displayed for His people in the wilderness. He led them out of their bondage in Egypt because of His limitless love for them. He parted the Red Sea and brought them through on dry land because of His limitless love for them. He provided manna from heaven for their sustenance because of His limitless love for them. He provided them victory over mightier armies because of His limitless love for them, and we could go on and on. He loved them, and loves us despite who we are, despite the many times we sin and disappoint Him, He always, out of His infinite love for us, continues to forgive us and give us another chance.

How often could we continue to forgive and love someone who has hurt us over and over and over again? Could we have a limit? Do we limit our love extended to others because of the hurt they've exposed us to? The answer is most likely yes. But God, no matter how many times we've hurt or disappointed Him, as the Israelites did time and again, still chooses to love us. He always does. He always will. That's a limitless love and it comes from God Himself, offered to us through His Son, Jesus Christ.

God's love is not only limitless, but His love is overarching! Overarching is described as being dominating or all-embracing; it's comprehensive. It's also described as covering everything and everyone.

God's overarching love, thankfully, embraces or covers all aspects of our lives. It even dominates our sin.

His love is so far-reaching that it *"covers over a multitude of sins." 1 Pet.4:8. NIV* His loves cleanses us from our sins. No matter what sin we've caused and how deep a wound it's caused, His love reaches to the depths of that sin and covers it over. He forgives it. He forgets about it.

This doesn't mean that God excuses the sin in our lives, because He doesn't. He forgives those sins when we ask Him to, when we repent. Sin isn't excused and God doesn't look the other way, but He covers it over and removes it from us. Psalm 103:12 says, *"as far as the east is from the west, so far has he removed our transgressions from us." NIV.* That's an overarching love indeed.

There is nowhere we could go that will separate us from the love of God. It's that overarching. Paul even addresses this type of love in Romans when he asks if anything in this life or beyond can separate us from God's love. *"Can anything ever separate us from Christ's love?" Rom 8:35A.*This is a crucial question posed by Paul. Is there somewhere we could go or something we could do that is out of the reach of God's love, where we are concerned? That's a fair question Paul pondered.

Paul continued, *"Does it mean He no longer loves us if we have trouble or calamity, or are persecuted, or hungry, or destitute, or in danger, or threatened with death?" V.35B.* Paul pretty much covers it all when he asks if trouble or calamity will stop God's reach into those areas of our lives that are difficult and troublesome. Paul even quotes the Word of God to perhaps presume that God's love isn't evident when he quoted Psalm 44:22 which says, *"For your sake we are killed every day; we are being slaughtered like sheep." NLT*

Paul, after asking himself these important thought-provoking questions, comes to the conclusion that God's love reaches and overarches into all areas of our lives. Nothing can separate us from

His overarching love when he concluded in verses 38 and 39, *"And I am convinced that nothing can ever separate us from God's love. Neither death nor life, neither angels nor demons, neither our fears for today nor our worries about tomorrow — not even the powers of hell can separate us from God's love. No power in the sky above or in the earth below — indeed, nothing in all creation will ever be able to separate us from the love of God that is revealed in Christ Jesus our Lord." NLT*

Wow! That is an overarching love indeed. There is absolutely nothing in this life or beyond that can separate us from God's love poured out through His Son, Jesus Christ, Paul concluded. Christ is God's overarching love that needs to be evidenced in our lives every day and He wants to evidence it in our lives now.

God's overarching love reaches down into the depths of our hearts, a place so many don't want to travel, to remove anything there that's not of Him. It may be painful, but if God's overarching love will remove it and replace it with His love, then it's worth it.

God's love is also victorious. Yes, there is victory in love! The love of Christ was shown upon the cross at Calvary when He was slain for our sins. Initially it seemed that death and sin had conquered Him, that death's sting injected into our Lord and Savior was victorious. He died on the cross at Calvary, His body broken and bloodied for our sins. He was removed and placed in a tomb, a dark and foreboding resting place. All seemed hopeless. All seemed lost. The enemy, Satan, appeared to have finally won the battle he had waged from eternity past.

What victory was there in Jesus' death? There was no victory if He stayed buried. But He didn't! On the third day after He was buried, the selfless love that He displayed by leaving the perfect confines of heaven to come down to earth to dwell among a sinful people and allowing Himself to be nailed to a cross was on full display again.

The love Jesus has for all of us empowered Him to raise Himself from the dead! Jesus' resurrection from the dead finally conquered death and sin. Sin no longer had power over us. He was victorious over the sin that plagues us.

When love permeates our entire being, as it did Jesus, we will always be victorious! Always! Let's look at it this way: When Jesus took the sins of the world upon His body and died upon the cross, did His perfect love end there too? The answer is a resounding NO! In fact, it was that perfect love that conquered sin. It was that perfect love emanating throughout His very being that conquered sin! It always will. Sin couldn't conquer love and never will. Love will always conquer sin.

If Jesus wasn't love, we would never have victory. That's why the church needs the antidote of love injected into its bloodstream because, when it is, it will conquer all, even death! God's love is victorious and it was fully revealed in His Son's resurrection. *"Death is swallowed up in victory."* *"O*

Death, where is your sting? O Hades, where is your victory?" "The sting of death is sin, and the strength of sin is the law. But thanks be to God, who gives us the victory through our Lord Jesus Christ." 1 Cor.15:54B-57. NKJV

Love gives us the victory and Jesus is our perfect example of that victorious love. God's love doesn't condemn us. It frees us from the sin in our lives so we can walk in victory. That's a crucial aspect of God's love. It frees us. It enables us to live a victorious life. The world's love is a love that condemns. That's why the world's love isn't a true lasting love, but a false love stored up by the enemy to confuse and render us incapable of allowing God's love to be injected into our lives and the life of the church. *"There is therefore now no condemnation for those who are in Christ Jesus." Rom. 8:1 NKJV*

God's love is victorious simply because He is for us and not against those who acknowledge Him as Lord and Savior. Romans 8 details God's overarching and victorious love. It was referenced earlier to

The Attributes of God's Love

describe His overarching love, but now let's look at how God's love is victorious in our walk.

Since God's love is victorious, what could separate us from that love? He is for us, right? So we have victory then? Yes. We have victory. *"If God is for us, who can be against us?"* Certainly not God, who did not even withhold His own Son, but offered Him up for us all. He gave us His Son, so will He not also freely give us all things? Who will accuse God's chosen people? God Himself declares them not guilty! Who, then, will condemn them? Not Christ Jesus, who died, or rather, who was raised to life and is at the right-hand side of God, pleading with Him for us! Who then can separate us from the love of Christ? Can trouble do it, or hardship, or persecution or hunger or poverty or danger or death? As the Scripture says, *"For your sake we are in danger of death at all times; we are treated like sheep that are going to be slaughtered. No, in all these things we have complete victory through Him who loved us." Rom.8:31-37. GNB*

There is absolutely no condemnation in God's love. There is complete and lasting victory. We can bask in that victorious love because God gave us His one and only Son so, as the Scripture points out, why would He withhold anything good from us? He gave us His best — His Son! So if He freely gives to those He loves, then He freely gives us His love in totality, withholding nothing from us.

Imagine what the church in America could conquer with God's love expressed today within the church walls and in our communities. No matter what financial hardship we face, or persecution and condemnation from the world, or poverty, or danger on every side, none of it matters. We are victorious! Persecution and condemnation must never be allowed in the church, because there will be no love, and if there's no love, there's no victory. They must stay outside the church with the world and not be brought into the church.

We should bring the complete victory of God's love into our communities. The last verses describe us as **more than conquerors** and that we have **complete victory** in Christ Jesus. The Free Dictionary describes a conqueror as someone who defeats or subdues by force, especially by force of arms. It's also described as "to overcome or surmount by physical, mental, or moral force, to be victorious, to win." Victory is defined as successes in a struggle against difficulties or an obstacle, or the state of having triumphed.

Because of Christ's love, we are more than conquerors and have complete victory! Wow! We conquer sin by the force of love. We overcome. We don't need to raise physical arms to subdue the enemy of sin; simple, perfect love will do that. If God's love is displayed in our lives on a daily basis, the people with whom we display that love will be the ones who are disarmed by the power of love!

Love disarms and subdues the hatred and bigotry and judgmental attitudes, the unforgiving attitudes, the resentments, and bitterness, and everything else that is sinful. None of that could ever stand up to or conquer love. Never. But the Scripture says we are MORE than conquerors! That means that God's love will completely eradicate any remnant of sin that remains. It will be wiped out, gone, never to return again. Our victory is complete. It lacks nothing. It has triumphed. No more victory is needed in our struggle because it is complete.

Victorious love makes something whole or perfect, so having that complete victory is making the victorious love whole and complete, and lacking nothing. We can never imagine what God's love will accomplish if it begins to sweep across America's landscape. God's love is victorious so we need to begin, as a church, walking in that victory afforded us through the love of Jesus Christ!

God's love is also eternal. It's without end. His love stretches from eternity past to eternity future. It is timeless and can't be measured. His love for us is so pure and immeasurable; we can't even begin to understand it. We can't. We're finite beings who could never grasp the eternal love He has for us.

If God's very essence is love and He is an eternal God, than His love is eternal. *"For the Lord is good and His love endures forever. His faithfulness continues through all generations." Ps. 100:5 NIV* His love will never end. It will always be present and has everlasting endurance. Our love, outside of God's love, will never endure because it isn't a pure and true, everlasting love. Our so-called love will die, but God's will be sustained forever. If His love is eternal, then His love forgives our sins. His love blots them out and will continue to endure.

The beginning of Psalm 90 talks about the everlasting God when the psalmist states, *"Lord, you have been our dwelling place in all generations. Before the mountains were brought forth, or ever you had formed the earth and the world, even from everlasting to everlasting, you are God." NKJV* Before even the earth and world was created, God was and is. He is from everlasting to everlasting, without beginning or end, and that is the kind of love that is expressed in Him.

No church will ever fail when it implements the eternal love instilled in our hearts through the love of Jesus Christ. If the church is going to be a powerful force in America today through the love of God poured out and into the hearts of His people through the acceptance of Jesus Christ's sacrificial death upon the cross, then what are we to do with this love? How must we apply it? A love that is limitless, overarching, victorious, and eternal is so overwhelmingly powerful, so indescribable, and so matchless: how can we apply this life-saving and life-changing force? Let's look at God's Word for more insight.

Chapter 19
Applying God's Love

When Jesus was asked in Mark 12:28 which is the greatest commandment of all, He answered, *"And you shall love the Lord your God out of and with your whole heart and out of and with all your soul (your life) and out of and with all your mind (with your faculty of thought and your moral understanding) and out of and with all your strength." AMP* Jesus also mentions that there is but one God and one God alone.

Jesus said that we are to love God with our entire being, withholding nothing from Him. Every fiber of our being, which includes our soul and mind, everything must be sold out for God. He doesn't say to share some of ourselves with the world and the other part of us with Him. We must give Him our ALL, our everything.

Since God is love and He commands that we love Him with our lives, we cannot fulfill that command unless we receive His love for us first. We cannot give what we do not have. The love Jesus is describing is that agape love described before, the love freely given in return with no conditions, no strings attached. *"We love because He first loved us." 1 Jn 4:19 NIV*

We can only love God in return with the love He has extended to us. We have no love to return to God that doesn't emanate from Him. And if it doesn't emanate from His being, then it isn't love at all. It's a fake, unreal, "I'll love you if you do what I want you to do" false love. We simply love because He has first loved us. And that is the first and most important commandment issued by Jesus.

Once we have received His love and love Him in return with the same love He has given us, by sacrificing our lives unto Him, then we are ready to share that love with the world that so desperately needs His love to be poured out into their hearts through us. That leads us to the second commandment Jesus talks about in Mark 12.

In verse 31 in the Amplified Bible, Jesus says, *"The second is like this, You shall love your neighbor as yourself. There is no other commandment greater than these."* We will look at this commandment in greater detail because of how we treat our neighbors: our friends, co-workers, strangers, the homeless, the widowed, the orphaned, the ex-convict, the people we come into contact with on a daily basis.

1 John is an excellent example of the biblical love we are to have with God and then with one another. In chapter 4, John describes how we can actually know God through our love for our brothers and sisters, inside and outside the church. Let's first look at verse 7. *"Beloved, let us love one another, for love is of God; and everyone who loves is born of God and knows God." NIV*

John says that we must love one another because love is OF God. This proves that true biblical love comes from God alone, and if we love God we will also love one another. He also says that when we practice this true love then we will know God, because God is love. However, *"He who does not love does not know God, for God is love." V.8 NIV*

For us to know God, we must first love Him with the love shown through Jesus, and then share that love with others. John continues in verse 9, *"In this the love of God was manifested toward us, that God has sent His only begotten Son into the world, that we might live through Him." NIV* God demonstrated and displayed His love for us by giving up His only Son to die a death that would allow us to live that life of love through Him. It was the greatest love of all that was on display for us to receive through faith. There was and never will be a greater act of love than Jesus Christ's display of His love for us with His death upon the cross, and we now have the power to share that amazing love with others.

It was pure love in action, based upon our will to receive that love. He was that perfect sacrifice of love for us. *"In this is love, not that we loved God, but that He loved us, and sent his Son to be the propitiation for our sins." V.10 NIV* Jesus' death was the propitiation or fulfillment of God's love for us. God was satisfied with His Son's death. God's wrath directed at us due to our sinful lives was actually directed at His Son, as He became sin for us. That is true love. A love that is evidenced by One willing to give up His own Son and watch Him die in the place where you and I belong is the most powerful, limitless, overarching, victorious, and eternal love that was ever displayed.

It is through this love that John is led to say, *"Beloved, if God so loved us, we ought to love one another." V.11 NIV.* He is saying that if God has shown us His love in this way, then we should be extending this love to each other in the same way God extended it to us.

Earlier in chapter 3 of the book of 1 John, he says that we can see who the children of God are and who the children of the devil are. It's simply those who practice righteousness and love one another are those who display God's love, and those who don't practice righteousness and hate their brother are those who belong to the devil, and display his love or what they think is love.

"None of those who are children of God continue to sin, for God's very nature is in them; and because God is their Father, they cannot continue to sin. This is the clear difference between God's children and the Devil's children: all who do not do what is right or do not love others are not God's children." 1Jn. 3:9-10. GNB. The ability to live righteous lives and to do what is right in this life is only obtained by receiving the righteousness of God, through our acceptance of His love extended to us. His righteousness and very nature are within us, therefore we cannot continue to sin. He doesn't say we'll never sin, but it won't be habitual or continuous because His love dwells

within us. This gives us the strength to overcome the sin in our lives because His love is victorious.

There is a clear difference between those who belong to God and those who belong to the devil, because the world's love emanates from the devil and God's love comes from His kingdom in heaven. As we look deeper into what the world or the god of this world offers us, we realize it is not pure love, but the love that's founded in self-centeredness. The world's love is all about our emotions. It's based on how we feel at any given moment. It's based on what is done for my benefit and, if it's done for me in the way I approve, then I'll extend my love. If it's something that's done on my behalf but I don't approve of that action, then I'll withhold my love from that person. It's selfish and simply based on how I feel. Sometimes I feel good and other times I don't. We vacillate with our emotions, but true biblical love is consistent —always. Biblical love isn't based upon my emotions or circumstances at any certain time. Biblical love is always evident, no matter the circumstance.

Biblical love is a willful and purposeful commitment that's not based upon our emotions. That is a huge difference. Biblical love and worldly love are too different to be compared. God willed, purposed and committed His Son to die for us. It was a sacrificial love. It wasn't based upon God's emotions or because we loved Him or did something to earn or deserve that love. God sent His Son simply because of His love for us. He has a desire for us to return that love to Him and to share that love with others.

Romans 5:8 says, *"But God demonstrates His own love for us in this: while we were still sinners, Christ died for us." NIV.* God acted out or demonstrated His love for us specifically by sending Jesus to die for us. There was nothing good within us to deserve that love. There was nothing we could have done to earn His love. It wasn't based upon the world's view of love, but God's view. We were sinners who lived for the devil, who defied and cursed God at every opportunity, yet He still loved us.

The Bible also describes different kinds of love that exist in the world, and they are phileo and eros love. The phileo love is the brotherly love we extend to someone else. Jesus attempted to get Peter to respond to him in the agape form of love when, in John 21:15-17, Jesus asked him if he loved Him. *"When they had eaten, Jesus said to Simon Peter, Simon, son of John, do you love (agape) me more than these [others do — with reasoning, intentional, spiritual devotion, as one loves the Father]? He said to Him, Yes, Lord, You know that I love (phileo) You [that I have a deep, instinctive, personal affection for you, as for a close friend]."* AMP

Jesus asked him two more times, and Peter became saddened and hurt because Jesus repeatedly asked him if he loved Him. Jesus did this because He tested Peter's love for Him. Did Peter at that moment have an agape love for Jesus? No, he didn't. Peter did love Jesus, but he loved Him as one has a brotherly affection for someone. He loved Him as a friend, a brother. Jesus desired a deeper, more committed love, a love He would pour out for Peter and for us. What He desired from Peter He desires from us too: a pure, willful, committed love unto Him forever, even if it means our own death.

Peter would develop that agape love for Jesus because his life was martyred for Him. The brotherly love Peter had for Jesus that developed into an agape love is possible for us, too. It's as if Jesus is asking us in the church what He asked Peter. Do we love Him more than a brother or friend? Are we sold out for Him as He's sold out for us? Do we love Jesus even if it means a separation from our own family and friends? Do we have that agape love that, if we ever faced death for His sake, we would willingly die for Him? Sadly, many of us within the church claim we love Jesus as Peter did, but only as a brother and nothing more. The first sign of persecution from the world and we become quiet or afraid and we run away from Him by running away from the persecution.

Did Jesus run away from us when He was persecuted? In the Garden of Gethsemane, when He prayed a prayer that the cup He was given by God be removed from Him, did He allow Himself to walk away? He concluded to let the Lord's will be done and not His will. Was it easy for Jesus to know a terrible suffering awaited Him? He knew the type of death He would face, which would temporarily separate Him from His Father, but did He walk away because the situation was too difficult to face? No, because godly love was on display and, when on display, will always strengthen us for all the persecutions, trials, and tribulations we will ever face in this life. Jesus displayed that love by deciding to go forward with the suffering and death that awaited Him, because of His love for us. If His will was injected into the situation, Jesus would not have gone to the cross for us. He would not have shown the agape love, but only a phileo love towards us. Brotherly love wouldn't have led Him to the cross, and brotherly love won't lead us out of our sin.

However, Jesus didn't show phileo love. He made a willful, purposeful decision that wasn't based upon His emotions at that time or He would not have followed through and suffered the terrible death He did. It was entrenched in His deep agape love for you and me! And it was that love that sent Him to the cross.

The eros love that exists is a sexual love. It's a love based in lust for someone or a sexual love we have for our spouse. There is a place for eros love within the confines of marriage, but not outside of that. However, the world, through Satan, has perverted eros love and believes that pure, sexual love is true love, but that simply isn't true.

Chapter 20

Worldly Love vs. Godly Love

Biblical love doesn't mesh with worldly love. John used an example of what happens when someone whose love comes from the world comes into contact with someone whose love comes from God. The example comes from two brothers found in the Bible in Genesis, Cain and Abel. John uses them as a reminder that worldly love and godly love are polar opposites. One cannot mix with the other. He uses this example because we spend most of our time in the world. We even bring the world into our homes on a daily basis through workplace issues and our exorbitant amount of time watching everything on television, from reality shows to violent-themed shows. Biblical love then begins to mesh with worldly love and our godly lenses become darkened and skewed by the world so we cannot separate biblical love from worldly love.

In Genesis chapter 4, we see the story of Cain and Abel, both born into sin through their parents, Adam and Eve. They had their sin nature, but Abel received God's love and utilized that love in his personal relationship with God and in his personal character. However, Cain chose to jettison God's love in favor of the world's love, which is sin.

The story tells of how both brothers brought an offering to God, but only Abel's was sufficient and accepted of God and Cain's wasn't. Why? Because Abel was totally sold out to God. He had received His love and returned that love with his whole mind, body, soul, and spirit. He gave God his all, his very best, and was obedient. Abel knew what it was like to return the love God had showered upon him. Cain, on the other hand, only gave God what he wanted to give Him, what he felt he should give to God. He only gave a part of himself and what he thought was sufficient for God and that was unacceptable.

We don't exhibit true love to God unless we give Him our all in an act of obedience and love. God had accepted Abel's offering but had rejected Cain's. This act of rejection had infuriated Cain and God recognized this when He said, *"Why are you angry? And why has your countenance fallen? If you do well, will you not be accepted? And if you do not do well, sin lies at the door. And its desire is for you, but you should have rule over it." Gen. 4:6-7 NKJV*

God so desires to accept us, but we need to do well by Him. What did God mean when He said that Cain didn't do well? He simply didn't love God in the way He desired that he love Him. He required Cain's offering to be that of total obedience to Him. He wanted Cain's true and unadulterated love as Abel had given Him, but Cain refused. Perhaps his sin so skewed his perception of what God's love really required that he thought he loved God.

The world and its sin so stain and shut out God's love when they permeate our lives that we can't know what true love and devotion to God really mean. We may think we know what His love is, but we really don't. Isn't the church in America like that today? Haven't we become like Cain in the church and not the Abel God desires? Don't we give unto God what we think He should have in our lives and draw the line in certain areas, refusing to let Him in and still expect Him to accept us and what we offer Him?

God's focus wasn't on Cain's offering but on the attitude of his heart. His focus was on Cain's lack of true devotion to Him. He desired that Cain's life be a life sacrificed unto Him, borne out of his love for the Father. True love is a lifelong sacrifice that He desires of us. But Cain's heart wasn't the same as his brother's heart, and that's why God warned Cain as He warns us that sin lies at the door of our heart, desiring to enter it, and all of the sin and destruction that come with it.

As stated earlier, sin has crept into the church through the door of our hearts. It no longer sits at the door as He warned Cain, because it sits inside the church and has taken hold of the hearts of the people as it did Cain. It drains the love of God from us as it did Cain, rendering him and us incapable of understanding and receiving God's love for us. His warning steeped in love was to save us from his and our impending heartache and disaster.

God warned that sin's desire is for us, but we must rule over it. How could we do that? We do it by applying God's love to our lives. *"Above all, love each other deeply, because love covers over a multitude of sins." 1 Pet.4:8 NIV.* The Amplified Bible states, *"Above all things have intense and unfailing love for one another, for love covers a multitude of sins [forgives and disregards the offenses of others]."*

The love of God displayed in our lives will blot out and erase our sins and allow us to forgive the sins and offenses committed against us by others. However, we must love each other deeply. We need to have an intense, burning, and unfailing love for one another. Cain didn't display God's love. He didn't allow God's love to cover his sin, but he allowed his sin to control him, thereby draining any love he had shown to God before. His sin intensified instead of love, which resulted in the murder of his own flesh and blood.

Had Cain simply acknowledged his sin and repented of it, he would have not only received forgiveness from God, but His unfailing love as well, because love forgives sin. Sin would have had no effect on Cain anymore, but he chose to reject God's love, as so many do in the church today.

Instead of recognizing the sins in our lives and repenting of them and getting right with God, we get angry and hurt, leave the church and go to another one that will accept our anger and hurt, or perhaps we stop going altogether. Where is God's love displayed? How can He eradicate the sin in our lives with His love when we won't let Him?

Worldly Love vs. Godly Love

There are too many church hoppers and those who leave the church because of their hurts. God is willing to pour His love into our hurting hearts, but we won't let Him. Didn't God desire to forgive Cain as He desires to forgive us? Didn't God want to pour out His forgiving love into Cain's heart as He wants to do for us? The answer is yes!

God had given Cain another chance to make things right. He didn't reject him forever, but he rejected his half-hearted approach to Him. He even told him what He saw wrong with his life and what he had to do to get himself right, to prepare himself to be accepted by God. God does the same for the church today. He hasn't given up on us. He still desires a pure and loving relationship with us and still has that open invitation to the church in America today. There is still time to turn it around. He hasn't given up on us yet.

Cain chose sin over God's love, but we don't have to do the same. Despite God's punishment upon Cain for his evil act of murder, He still loved him and protected him by promising to take vengeance upon those who would try to hurt Cain. Wow! What an amazing love that is! He still protected him by setting a mark upon him, a hedge around him so to speak, so He could protect him.

God still protects us, but there are consequences to our sin. Cain wouldn't receive the full blessings God had desired for Him. He didn't say He wouldn't bless him, He said he would withhold some of His blessings from him. Cain wouldn't be able to enjoy the fruit of his labors and would be a nomad, a wanderer in life, always running from God.

Cain also never repented of his sin before God. He was self-absorbed. He was engaged in his own self-indulgent needs as he continued to worry about his own fate and never expressed remorse over killing his own brother. Sin is always turned inward. It focuses on our own needs and desires because its desire is always for us, to gain control over us.

The fact that Cain lacked a repentant heart was the reason he would never fully realize God's love for him. If he repented of his sins before God, he would have been able to recover from his sin by first receiving God's love through His act of forgiveness, receiving a new, transplanted heart, and then extending God's love to others around him. Are we the same way? Do we refuse to repent of our sin, yet expect God to fully bless us? God was still merciful to Cain despite His righteous judgment for his sinful behavior, and He's merciful to us. But He has so much more for us, as He did for Cain, if we are just willing to look beyond our own selfish and fleshly desires and take responsibility for our actions by repenting and receiving God's forgiveness. His forgiveness is love in action, and that's what He wants to do in and through us. Cain, sadly, never realized that powerful love and, sadly, many in the church don't either, and perhaps never will.

Cain lamented his punishment as too great for him to bear and that God would not allow him into His presence. What a great punishment indeed, but

His mercy on Cain was far greater than any punishment God had pronounced upon him.

Although there are consequences to our sin, God does indeed forgive and will still bless His people in the church today because of the sacrificial death of Jesus Christ. Since His love *"covers a multitude of sins,"* we begin to receive the blessings He has for us because we are His children, and His love for us will always be there; it will never fail.

Jesus is also standing at the door of the church and wants to be invited in, and for the unwanted guest of sin to be thrown out. His love wants to grip the church and take up residence each week in the hearts of the people. He wants His love to permeate the pulpit in the form of the truth of the Gospel. He wants His love to permeate the unforgiveness, resentment, jealousy, hatred, bitterness, anger, and any other sin that permeates the heart of the church. We need to invite Him in and welcome Him into the life of the church, but we need to give Him our all, holding nothing back. It must be on His terms and not ours. We can't display love one day and not the next. It's not a light switch that we can turn on and off like our emotions, but it must be willing to receive a daily dose of God's love for it to be effective and eternally lasting.

Earlier, one of the seven churches described in Revelation was the Lukewarm Church. It's the church with a half-hearted approach to God, as Cain had with his life. One day the church is blazing with its love for God and the next time that love isn't evident at all. Jesus describes this church as being neither hot nor cold but lukewarm.

We have many lukewarm churches in America today that don't need to be that way. It's a church that's confused because it's not sure how Christ's love should be displayed, and it renders itself useless to God. He said that He will vomit them out of His mouth. This is a very vivid description of His rejection of the church and His people. However, Jesus is still standing at the door of the church and knocks and still wants to come into the church and have fellowship with her. He describes His relationship with the church as one who has dinner with His guests.

There is also another church that Jesus describes in Revelation chapter 2, and it's the Loveless Church. It's described by Jesus as a church that labored hard for Him. It's that church with the great music ministry, children's ministry, and youth group. It's a church that has many works and even fruit it has produced as a result of its labor. It has persevered and has been patient. It's even the church that won't bear with those operating in sin, those who are evil. However, Jesus still had a charge against this church.

This church, by all accounts, seemed to be a thriving church. There are wonderful ministries evident in this church and they are experiencing a major growth, so what could be wrong? What's missing from this church that Jesus has a problem with it? This is what He said: *"But I have this [one charge to make] against you: that you have left (abandoned) the love that you had at first [you have deserted Me, your first love]. Remember then from what heights you have fallen. Repent (change the inner man to meet God's will) and do the works you did previously [when you first knew the Lord], or else I will visit you and remove your lampstand from its place, unless you change your mind and repent." Rev. 2:4-5 AMP*

This church at Ephesus that Jesus was referring to was a church lacking in His love. They had not obeyed Jesus' command to love God totally and completely, as Jesus referenced in Matthew 22. The church was the one that Paul had praised in Ephesians 1 as the church that first had faith in Christ and extended that love to all the saints, the people within the church. He then later encouraged them in chapter 4 to grow in their love for one another.

This is the same church Jesus had referenced as abandoning Him. It's impossible for a church to grow in a way pleasing to God without its love for Him first evidenced; otherwise it's not true love. Sin crept into that church and forced out God's love, a love not welcomed anymore. Jesus commanded that they repent and return to Him, to recapture their love for Him by returning to their first works, which were what? Works labored and entrenched in love! He was referring to what Paul evidenced in the church earlier. He had commended them for having a love for the saints and encouraged them to grow in their love for one another, but they lost that, and too many churches today have lost their first love too — Jesus Christ, but He stills says we have the opportunity to return to Him. It isn't too late!

As Cain had an unrepentant heart and couldn't return to God because he wasn't willing to receive His love, so too have many churches. We need to first recognize the sin in our lives and ask for forgiveness; otherwise we lose out on Christ's forgiving love. Why else would He command us to repent first before we could ever return to Him? Because it's impossible for us to receive that love and to continue in that love when our hearts are entrenched in sin. We rid ourselves of the sin and then we receive His love.

Worldly Love vs. Godly Love

Whether it's a compromising church, a corrupt church, a loveless church, a dead church, or a lukewarm church, they all lack one key ingredient for their current and eternal success, and that's love. Love will carry us on into eternity because love is eternal; it's without end. The two churches Jesus had no criticism for were the persecuted and faithful churches, because they were steeped in His love. He didn't require repentance because love was evident in their churches, despite some hardships, despite persecution from the world outside. They endured because love endures and the church in America needs to do the same.

Chapter 21

Love Is the Answer

*L*et's take a final look at love in action as described in 1 Corinthians 13. If the church in America can apply the agape love described here in their churches, we will receive the crown of life that awaits us on our Judgment Day.

"Love is patient, love is kind. It does not envy, it does not boast, it is not proud. It does not dishonor others, it is not self-seeking, it is not easily-angered, and it keeps no record of wrongs. Love does not delight in evil but rejoices with the truth. It always protects, always trusts, always hopes, and always perseveres. Love never fails. And now these

three remain: faith, hope, and love. But the greatest of these is love." 1 Cor. 13:4-8A, 13NIV

Because God is love, He encompasses all of these acts of love within His very being and extends this agape love and all its accompanying benefits to each one of us. This is true love in action. The Bible contains many people who demonstrated this love in their lives, with the greatest example of that love personified in Jesus Christ.

First, love is patient. This is listed first because without patience it will be difficult to fulfill all the other characteristics of love, because patience suffers long. Patience is there when difficulty and trials and circumstances overwhelm us. Patience in those difficult times is crucial because it exhibits more growth in our love. Exhibiting love through patience produces so many benefits to us and those around us. Experiencing patience through love is a precious gift to give and to receive for ourselves.

The Scripture teaches, *"But we also glory in our sufferings, because we know that suffering produces perseverance (patience); perseverance, character; and character, hope. And hope does not put us to shame, because God's love has been poured out into our hearts through the Holy Spirit, who has been given to us." NIV.* Hope is the end result when patience is sown in love.

When we suffer in this life because of a physical ailment, or we suffer because someone hurts us, we need to be patient in love; otherwise our character, the temperament or personality created by God and instilled within us cannot develop. If character isn't developed, we'll lose hope, the hope being Jesus Christ.

The Scripture in James is a great example of patience. *"Therefore be patient, brethren, until the coming of the Lord. See how the farmer waits for the precious fruit of the earth, waiting patiently for it until it receives the early and latter rain. You also be patient." 4:7-8A. NKJV.*

James was referring to the cruel treatment and injustices we endure in this life. If we exhibit godly patience sown in love, like the farmer sows his seed and patiently waits for the fruit of his labors, so should we wait patiently on the Lord, because He will deliver us in due time. We'll experience the fruit of patience when we love one another and bear with one another.

Love is kind. Kindness is described in Wikipedia as a behavior marked by ethical characteristics, a pleasant disposition, and concern for others. Kindness is a behavior; it's a way of life for God as it should be for us. It is a genuine concern for other people. Kindness even needs to be extended to our enemies as Jesus said, *"But love your enemies, do good, and lend, hoping for nothing in return; and your reward will be great, and you will be sons of the Most High. For He is kind to the unthankful and evil." Lk. 6:35. NKJV.*

Kindness to others is crucial if we want our great reward. Yes, it is possible to love those who hurt us because Jesus does and we could too. Of course it isn't easy, and that's why we need Christ's strength to extend kindness to those who hurt us, those we'd even consider our enemies. He promises that our rewards will be great if we practice kindness rooted in love.

We don't just receive the reward of heaven, which is awesome in itself, but He will bestow upon us much more than even eternal life in heaven with Him, because He knows extending kindness to those who hurt is nearly impossible without His love flowing out of us. We do it simply to please Him.

Extending forgiveness to those who hurt us is rooted in kindness too. *"And become useful and helpful and kind to one another, tenderhearted (compassionate, understanding, loving-hearted), forgiving one another [readily and freely], as God in Christ forgave you." Eph. 4:32 AMP.*

Forgiveness is an act of kindness. Extend the gift of forgiveness today. It's one of the greatest acts of love rooted in kindness. *"Pardon, I pray You, the iniquity of this people according to the greatness of Your mercy and loving-kindness, just as You have forgiven [them] from Egypt until now." Num. 14:19. AMP.*

God, according to His infinite mercy and kindness, forgives us our sins so we must extend that same kindness to others too.

Love does not envy or boast. True godly love doesn't desire the possessions of others and is happy for their accomplishments. *"A sound heart is the life of the flesh: but envy the rottenness of the bones." Prov. 14:30 KJV.* A sound heart is filled with pure godly love, and it doesn't envy. Jealousy will rot our bones and render us lifeless and useless to the kingdom of God because it is a sin borne out of a rotten, depraved heart.

Since envy emanates from a sinful heart, James warns against this debilitating sin in the church because of the tremendous confusion and hurt it leaves in its path every time. James considers this demonic, earthly and sensual. *"But if you have bitter jealousy (envy) and contention (rivalry, selfish ambition) in your hearts, do not pride yourselves on it and thus be in defiance of and false to the Truth. This [superficial] wisdom is not such as comes down from above, but is earthly, unspiritual (animal), even devilish (demoniacal). For wherever there is jealousy (envy) and contention (rivalry and selfish ambition), there will also be confusion (unrest, disharmony, rebellion) and all sorts of evil and vile practices." Jas. 3:14-16 AMP*

One of the main weapons the devil loves to deploy is the weapon of envy. If the seeds of envy could be planted in the hearts of the people, the fruit of confusion, rebellion, and a host of other evil thoughts and practices will spring forth and cause much havoc within the church. Envy caused Satan to defy God and be expelled from heaven and it will destroy the church too. Keep love in the church and envy and confusion will have no place. *"For God is not the author of confusion but of peace, as in all the churches of the saints." 1 Cor. 14:33 NKJV.* Where there's no envy but God's love, there will be peace.

Love also doesn't boast. Love doesn't brag. The Bible is clear that boasting is not of God and is sinful. There are many scriptural references regarding boasting, and one is found in Psalm 10:3 that says, *"For the wicked boasts of his heart's desire; he blesses the greedy and renounces the Lord." NKJV.* Boasting comes from a depraved heart, is only concerned about fulfilling its own desires, and has no room for God.

Love isn't prideful. Pride is enjoying satisfaction in our own abilities, strengths, and achievements without giving God any credit for them. It's putting ourselves on the throne and making everything in life about ourselves and not others. The Bible warns of the destruction that befalls those who are prideful. *"Pride goes before destruction, a haughty spirit before a fall." Prov. 16:18 NIV.*

Pride is very deceptive and has no place in the life of a church. Love will thank God for the abilities and position we have attained in this life. Love will be humble and not prideful, because pride will only destroy God's love when we allow it.

Love will not dishonor those who are loved. Love will honor, respect, and hold in high esteem the object of its love. Honor will not embarrass when love is employed. Never. Love will also not seek its own needs, desires, or goals, but the needs, desires, and goals of others. Imagine the church seeking to fulfill the needs and desires of other people instead of their own. They want to see the best in people and not the worst. They want to see them fulfill their God-given goals and dreams even if it puts on hold their own goals and dreams. That's a love that doesn't seek its own but seeks to assist others to fulfill their God-given dreams. "No one should seek their own good, but the good of others."1Cor.10:24 NIV.

Love isn't easily angered. This mirrors patience because anger easily aroused will lead to sin, but anger withheld will birth patience. Patience will help to dissolve anger. *"Do not be eager in your heart to be angry, for anger resides in the bosom of fools."*

Ecc. 7:9 NIV. "Cease from anger, and forsake wrath; Do not fret, it leads only to evildoing." Ps. 37:8 NIV. Anger resides or takes up residence in the hearts of those who are foolish. It will only lead to evil and hurting many people in its path.

Anger not resolved or cured with the power of love will only give the devil a foothold to wreak his havoc. *"Be angry, and yet do not sin; do not let the sun go down on your anger, and do not give the devil an opportunity." Eph. 4:26-27 NIV*

Love keeps no record of wrongs. How many times do we keep a record of those who have hurt us, not just recently, but going back many years? We harbor these records in our hearts, just waiting for the opportunity to throw it in their faces when others anger us. This isn't true godly love because godly love will forgive. It won't keep a record of the wrongs done to it. How many times could God make a charge against us and condemn us? Every time. God doesn't do it, though. *"As far as the east is from the west, so far has He removed our transgressions from us." Ps. 103:12 AMP.* He blots out our transgressions. Thankfully, He doesn't keep a record of our wrongs.

Paul took the Corinthian church to task because of their willingness to keep records of wrongs within the body of believers, and he wasn't happy about it. Members were filing lawsuits against each other and taking the matter before the pagan or worldly courts, instead of settling the matter among themselves with love and forgiveness.

"Dare any of you, having a matter against another, go to law before the unrighteous, and not before the saints? (Church)" 1 Cor. 6:1 NKJV He went on to say, *"If then you have judgments concerning things pertaining to this life, do you appoint those who are least esteemed by the church to judge?" V.4*

He was chastising them for bringing their wrongs against one another to the unbelievers. They were in fact making a mockery of their Christian faith for the entire world to see!

Paul urged them to deal with each other in love, and to carry that attitude with them at all times. He even said that we should rather be cheated than to be unloving. *"The very fact that you have lawsuits among you means you have been completely defeated already. Why not rather be wronged? Why not rather be cheated? Instead, you yourselves cheat and do wrong, and you do this to your brothers and sisters." Vv. 7-9A. NIV.* We should rather be cheated and wronged than to operate in anger and unforgiveness.

Jesus displayed His perfect act of love when He forgave those who crucified Him, when He said as He hung upon the cross, humiliated, bloodied, beaten, and mocked, *"Father, forgive them, for they do not know what they are doing." Lk 23:34 NIV.* He kept no records of wrongs committed against Him, and we should not either.

"Therefore as God's chosen people, holy and dearly loved, clothe yourselves with compassion, kindness, humility, gentleness and patience. Bear with each other and forgive one another if any of

you has a grievance against someone. Forgive as the Lord forgave you. And over all these virtues put on love, which binds them all together in perfect unity." Col. 3:12-14 NIV.

Of all the virtues listed: compassion, kindness, humility, gentleness, and patience, we are to wear or put on love. Love binds all of these virtues and all others together in perfect unity. Love must be worn so the church is unified and will forgive past mistakes or wrongs. Bury them and leave them buried, never to be dredged up again. Only those who wear love can wipe away any wrong done to them.

Love doesn't laugh when evil is committed, but love rejoices with and in the truth. Pilate, after Jesus was arrested, asked Him, *"What is truth?" Jn 18:38. NIV.* He responded to a statement Jesus made about Himself in the previous verse when He said, *"You say that I am a king. In fact, the reason I was born and came into the world is to testify to the truth. Everyone on the side of truth listens to me." V. 37B NIV.*

Love rejoices in the truth and the truth is Jesus Christ! To rejoice is to feel or show that you are very happy about something. Rejoicing in Jesus is a reason to be joyful and happy. *"And you shall know the truth, and the truth shall make you free." Jn 8:32. NKJV.* We rejoice because Jesus, the truth, has set us free from our sins that would send us to hell, but we are guaranteed eternity with Him because He is, *"the way, the truth, and the life." Jn 14:6A. NKJV.* Love rejoices in the truth!

We don't delight in evil. Those who serve the devil do. Evil and sin should grieve our souls and not bring us delight.

Love always protects. Love works to keep those we love under our protection or cover. It shelters and shields those they love. The Bible continually shows God's protection extended to us because He loves us, so He protects us. He watches out for us. God showed His protection to His people Israel throughout their journey in the wilderness and beyond, and it is still there today. We need to exercise protective love. We need to look out for each other in church and seek to protect them from being hurt and wounded.

God displayed His mighty protection to His people visibly, too. *"By the day the Lord went ahead of them in a pillar of cloud to guide them on their way and by night in a pillar of fire to give them light, so that they could travel by day or night." Ex.13:21 NIV.* His protection was evident twenty-four hours a day so they could see any roadblocks or dangers that might lie in wait for them.

God protects those He loves, and so should we. *"Because he has set his love upon Me, therefore will I deliver him; I will set him on high, because he knows and understands My name [has a personal knowledge of My mercy, love, and kindness — trusts and relies on Me, knowing I will never forsake him, no, never]." Ps. 91:14 AMP.*

When we love Him and extend that love to others, He promises to deliver us and set us on high, a place where we are above our problems and circumstances because we know Him, are familiar with Him. What an awesome promise of God when we protect one another in love.

Love always trusts. This doesn't mean that the person trusting is weak, fragile, and gullible. Love is always prepared to trust. Love believes in the other person because love is unconditional. We are not quick to judge someone we trust, but love will always consider the other person first and communicate that trust because trust communicates. Trust extends the benefit of the doubt to the object of love, no matter the situation. Even if someone you love has had a bad past or experiences, love will still trust and believe. What an awesome church we could become when we trust in others because that trust is grounded in love!

Love always hopes. Jesus is our hope! Paul called Jesus our hope. Peter stated that we should always be ready to explain the hope we have. *"But have reverence for Christ in your hearts, and honor Him as Lord. Be ready at all times to answer anyone who asks you to explain the hope you have in you." 1 Pet. 3:15 GNB.*

If Jesus, our hope, is inside us, dwelling within us through the Holy Spirit, then His love is in us too. Hope expects for the best and sees the best in others. Hope loves for the best in every situation, no matter how bad it seems. Love always hopes.

Love always perseveres. Love continues on unwavering, despite heartache, disappointment, and failure. Love never dies. It is always alive and always prevails. It is persistent in the darkest of times. Love doesn't quit when the going gets tough. When tough times occur in marriages, and they will, love will win out. When husband and wife pledge, "for better or for worse, for richer, for poorer, in sickness and in health, to love and to cherish; from this day forward until death do us part," they must take those words to heart. Those words spoken are grounded in the truth that love perseveres no matter how well or bad our marriages or relationships are going. It's not fleeting or temporary.

If there's true love evident in our marriages, lives, and in the church, we won't quit or walk away from what God has ordained, because love lasts and it lasts forever. Perseverance is a commitment. Jesus is our commitment and perfect example of enduring, persevering love. Jesus, at the Last Supper with His disciples and the same night in which He was betrayed into the hands of sinners, did this in John 13:1B, *"Having loved His own who were in the world, He loved them to the end." NIV.* Jesus' love didn't quit. His love didn't run away or hide or become angry and vengeful. No. His love for us persevered, no matter the cost, which was His very life given for ours when He died a terrible death upon the tree at Calvary.

"And let us run with endurance (perseverance) the race that is set before us, looking unto Jesus, the author and finisher of our faith, who for the joy that was set before Him endured (persevered) the cross, despising the shame, and has sat down at the right hand of the throne of God. For consider Him who endured (persevered) such hostility from sinners against Himself, lest you become weary and discouraged in your souls." Heb. 12:1B-3. NKJV

His love grounded in perseverance endured, and never gave up despite tremendous pressure and hostility. That's why we are to look to Jesus as our perfect example to stay the course and to endure, because love always endures. When we do, that joy will set in and love will have perfected itself within us because we didn't give up, and that's why the Scripture encourages us to follow Jesus' example. Otherwise we will become weary and discouraged and lose heart. We will give up on church, our marriages, and our relationships if love doesn't persevere.

Finally, Peter also encouraged the church to endure especially when we are grieved, hurt, or wronged and suffer for it. In 1 Peter 2:20, he says, *"For what credit is it if, when you are beaten for your faults, you take it patiently? But when you do good and suffer, if you take it patiently, this is commendable before God." NKJV*. Our perseverance because of the love of God rooted in our hearts, especially when wronged or persecuted, is pleasing and acceptable to God. Persevering love is true love.

Chapter 22

All Hope Is Not Lost

The church in America is sick and is surrounded by the pangs of death due to the sin (self-indulgent needs) that has engulfed it. It is slowly dying on its bed of iniquity because we'd rather serve our own sinful, selfish needs and desires than the needs and desires of others. We have allowed the sinful world and its practices to take root in our hearts and have thus brought those sins into the church, thus crippling it.

The poison of sin has taken root and has infiltrated the church body, but it isn't too late to save the church in America! There is still hope, and that hope is Jesus Christ. We need to return to our first love, but we first need to recognize our sinful practices and repent from them and then agree that a heart transplant is necessary. When God performs our heart transplant, He is then able to inject the dose of love into the veins of the church, a dose that will reinvigorate and raise the church from its bed of sickness and sin, so it can begin to reclaim its rightful place in America; a place where deliverances, signs and wonders, and power, and healing will once again take place. It will once again become the church that is the driving force for good in America; the proverbial shining light on a hill that penetrates the darkness of this world! The church in America will bring Jesus into the world and forever change it for His glory. It's not too late, church! But we must begin anew today! There is a cure! And that cure is LOVE, a certain pure, and life-changing love that will permeate America, a love that will be a sweet-smelling sacrifice unto God!

Sign on the dotted line and allow God, our perfect heart surgeon, begin the work He so desires to perform. The prophet Joel said this:

That is why the L ORD SAYS,
"Turn to me now, while there is time.
Give me your **hearts.**
Come with fasting, weeping, and mourning.
¹³ Don't tear your clothing in your grief,
but **tear your hearts** instead."
Return to the L ORD YOUR G OD,
for he is merciful and compassionate,
slow to get angry and filled with unfailing love.
He is eager to relent and not punish.
¹⁴ Who knows? Perhaps he will give you a reprieve,
sending you a blessing instead of this curse."
Joel 2:12-14A NLT

Our heart transplant will change our lives for eternity. We'll never be confined to our bed of sickness anymore! What an amazing and perfect prognosis our Surgeon gives us today: "You don't have to die. I will raise you from your bed of iniquity and save you and give you a new heart for My glory!" So what are we waiting for? Let Him begin the surgery today...

CPSIA information can be obtained at www.ICGtesting.com
Printed in the USA
BVOW11s1823250914

367964BV00004B/12/P